U

21905

Understanding Additives

Published by
Consumers' Association
and Hodder & Stoughton

Which? Books are commissioned and researched by
The Association for Consumer Research and published by
Consumers' Association, 2 Marylebone Road, London NW1 4DX
and Hodder & Stoughton, 47 Bedford Square, London WC1B 3DP

British Library Cataloguing in Publication Data

Understanding additives.
1. Food Additives
I. Consumers' Association II. Series
664'.06
ISBN 0-340-42557-1

Researched and compiled by Barbara Saunders
Consultant editor: Anna Bradley
Typography by Tim Higgins
Cover illustration by John Holder
Photoset by Paston Press, Loddon, Norfolk
Printed and bound in Great Britain by
Hazell Watson & Viney Limited,
Member of BPCC plc, Aylesbury, Bucks

Contents

Explanations of the work of the various organisations that appear throughout the book – the Food Advisory Committee (FAC) and the Committee on the Toxicity of Chemicals in Food, Consumer Products and the Environment (COT), for instance – are given in the Appendix on page 168.

Introduction

Over the past 30 years changes in food technology have revolutionised our food supply. Improved delivery, packaging and storage techniques have made it possible to supply a wide range of fresh fruits and vegetables throughout the year. The variety of processed products is as never before, and new methods of processing and preservation have led to the marketing of products as diverse as pot noodles and instant desserts. Whereas at the end of the Second World War, fewer than 1,000 different processed foods could be found in the shops, there are now about 10,000, and they form about three-quarters of the average diet.

Changes in food technology have been accompanied by extensive use of food additives to preserve, increase safety, aid processing, and improve the marketability of products. It has been estimated that the use of additives may have increased ten-fold between 1955 and 1985. Increasingly complex formulations of products have led to the use, within single products, of 'cocktails' of additives to achieve different complementary effects – for example adding strawberry flavour and pink colouring to create a strawberry flavour yoghurt; or using emulsifiers to mix oils with water and stabilisers to stop them separating again, as in salad cream or soft margarine; or exploiting one or more additive to enhance the effect of others, such as flavours or antioxidants.

Although over this period legislators gradually extended the controls on substances and drew up lists of about 330 permitted additives which could legally be added to foods, the changes in the use of additives went largely unnoticed by the British public, as manufacturers were not required to state in detail what went into products.

It is hardly surprising, therefore, that the introduction in 1986 of improved food labelling, which had been intended to provide people with better information about the ingredients and additives in processed food, caused a public outcry. People associated the appearance of 'E' numbers, a shorthand code for the additives approved for use in the European Community, with the introduction of new additives whose use they questioned. Misinformation, media coverage of potential safety hazards from some permitted additives, and worries about allergies all added to the confusion and concern. Indeed, for some people the new ingredients lists, rather than being helpful and informative, read more like a Government Health Warning. Some consumers reacted by complaining about the presence of so many unexpected, unknown and seemingly unnecessary ingredients in their food, and by changing their purchasing habits.

A survey* carried out for the Ministry of Agriculture, Fisheries and Food (MAFF) in 1986 showed that foods containing additives were second only to foods containing fat in the damage that people thought they would do to health. However, looking at the list of ingredients (where additives are listed) came fourth in the list of information that women looked for on food labels, after price, sell-by date and manufacturer's name. And while 52 per cent of the women claimed to have made changes in their buying and eating habits in the previous two years, only 16 per cent of them said that they were eating foods with fewer additives, while 50 per cent claimed to be eating more wholemeal bread, for example. All in all, it seems that concern about additives may not be being matched by appropriate action.

Some ingredients lists on the new labels, such as for biscuit assortments or processed meats, appeared long and unappetising. In many cases, lists of additives are far longer than the main ingredients, as this example for a low-calorie pineapple and grapefruit drink shows. Carbonated water, pineapple juice and grapefruit juice are processed with:

*Survey of Consumer Attitudes to Food Additives, Volume 1, 1987, HMSO.

> citric acid, flavouring, malic acid,
> acidity regulator (E331) monosodium citrate,
> artificial sweeteners aspartame/saccharin,
> tartaric acid, preservative (E211) sodium benzoate,
> ascorbic acid, stabiliser (E410) locust bean gum,
> colours (E104 quinoline yellow, E110 sunset yellow FCF)
> and antioxidants (E304 ascorbyl palmitate, E307 synthetic alpha tocopherol)

All of these are apparently necessary to produce a palatable, low-calorie drink, the main ingredient of which is water.

In response to public pressure, and their own desire to limit unnecessary ingredients, retailers and manufacturers made moves to limit the use of additives, and changed the formulations of many products accordingly. They started to question the ingredients in their products: what functions did they perform, and were they necessary?

More and more products with fewer and fewer additives are now being marketed. It seems that some manufacturers are trying to hunt with the hounds while running with the hare – claiming that an increasing number of food additives are necessary while at the same time producing an extended range of products without them. The position for consumers is unclear. Are additives still necessary?

To help people assess the situation – the ways additives are used in food products and the changes that are taking place in the food industry – we wrote to leading food manufacturers asking for details of their policy, and also had more detailed discussions with the leading retailers (see overleaf). Their replies are drawn on throughout the book.

Understanding additives

This book will help you decide what, if anything, you want to do about additives, by discussing the need for additives in general (Chapter 1), and their safety (Chapter 2). Some groups of additives are less necessary than others and some have presented more safety problems. Chapters 4–9, covering the different categories of additives, discuss these issues in general and give detailed information about some additives which have been associated with particular problems.

If, armed with all this information, you decide that you want to avoid foods containing certain additives, Chapter 3 will help you find out what is and is not labelled, and Chapter 10 will give you an idea of the policies of supermarkets, freezer food specialists and other chains towards additives.

Finally, if you want to find a particular additive but don't know where to start, the charts starting on page 172 will point you to the relevant pages.

Acknowledgements

The publishers would like to thank the retailers, distributors and manufacturers listed below for completing questionnaires, supplying information on their policies and practice, and in some instances for meeting to describe in detail the changes they were making. Without their assistance the book could not have been written in this form. The Ministry of Agriculture, Fisheries and Food, the British Industrial Biological Research Association (BIBRA), the Leatherhead Food Research Association, Consumers in the European Community Group (CECG) and the London Food Commission all gave valuable comments on drafts of the text, or some of the research on which it has been based. Their assistance is much appreciated. Any errors and omissions are, however, the responsibility of the publishers.

Retailers and distributors
Companies marked * participated in one or more meetings as well as supplying written information.

Argyll Foods (Presto)
* Bejam Freezer Food Centres Ltd
* The Boots Company plc
Budgen Ltd
* Co-Operative Wholesale Society Ltd
Gateway Foodmarkets Ltd
* Iceland Frozen Foods plc
* The Littlewoods Organisation plc

Marks and Spencer plc
* Wm Morrison Supermarkets plc
* Nurdin & Peacock Cash and Carry Ltd
* Safeway Food Stores Ltd
* J Sainsbury plc
* Spar (UK) Ltd
* Tesco Stores Ltd
* Waitrose Ltd

Manufacturers

Adams Foods Ltd
Allied Bakeries Ltd
Allied Breweries Management
  Services Ltd
Barker & Dobson Ltd
Bass plc
BEOCO Ltd
Bernard Matthews plc
Best Foods Division
Birds Eye Walls
Bowyers Ltd
Britvic Corona Ltd
Brooke Bond Oxo Ltd
Cadbury Ltd
Campbells UK Ltd
Carlsberg Brewery Ltd
Coca Cola
Colmans of Norwich Ltd
Dairy Crest Foods
Express Food Group Ltd
Freshbake
General Foods Ltd
Hazelwood & Co
H J Heinz Co Ltd
Hillsdown Ltd
HP Foods Ltd
Katie's Kitchen
The Kellogg Company Ltd
KP Foods Ltd
Kraft Foods Ltd
Ledbury Preserves 1928 Ltd
Lyons Bakery
Lyons Maid Ltd
Lyons Tetley Ltd
Manley Ratcliffe Ltd

Marietta Frozen Foods
Mars Confectionery Ltd
Mattessons Walls Ltd
McCain Foods Ltd
W L Miller & Sons Ltd
Napolina Ltd
The Nestlé Co Ltd
Palethorpes Ltd
Perrier (UK) Ltd
Pillsbury (UK) Ltd
Premier Brands UK Ltd
Princes Buitoni Ltd
Quaker Oats Ltd
Rank Hovis McDougall plc
Rayner & Co Ltd
Ross Foods Ltd
Rowntree Mackintosh
  Confectionery Ltd
St Ivel Ltd
Schweppes Great Britain Ltd
C Shippam Ltd
Snack Nut & Crisp Manufacturers'
  Association Ltd (SNACMA)
Soda Stream Ltd
Sovereign Chicken Ltd
Tate & Lyle Sugars
Trebor Ltd
UB Ltd
UB Frozen Foods
Unigate Dairies Ltd
Van Den Berghs & Jurgens Ltd
Weetabix Ltd
Weston Research Labs Ltd
Whitworths Holding Ltd

1
Do we need food additives?

Consumers have considerable doubts about the necessity of using additives. In the 1986 MAFF survey (see the Introduction), over two-thirds of the women taking part agreed with the statement that additives are an unnecessary ingredient; 37 per cent claimed to have bought 'additive-free' foods. When the women were asked why additives were used, 55 per cent said to lengthen shelf-life or make foods last longer, 54 per cent to colour foods or make them look better and 39 per cent to flavour foods.

The uses of food additives

Until now the need for additives has largely been determined by the functions which they can fulfil, and the types of food in which they perform satisfactorily. Additives are ingredients, not usually regarded or used as foods themselves, but which are used in or on food to affect its keeping qualities, appearance, taste, texture or other properties, or to assist in processing. They are normally used at low or very low levels, but their importance is far greater than the amounts used would suggest.

Additives have long been used in the preservation of food. The Romans used saltpetre to preserve meat and sulphur to prevent the oxidation of wine. By the start of the twentieth century, about 50 additives were used for limited purposes. They included alum to whiten bread, formalin to preserve milk, arsenic sulphide to give Bath buns their yellow colour, and red lead to colour cheese. Although there were no specific regulations governing the use of additives, from 1875 the Sale of Food and Drugs Act required that food should be safe and 'of the nature, substance and quality' demanded by the consumer.

A landmark in the history of additives occurred in 1925 when the use of boric acid in food was banned under the Preservatives Regulations of that year, by which time the subject was already controversial. Consumer concern has risen with the numbers of additives in use.

Today, as many as 3,800 additives are used for many functions, of which 24 categories are covered by regulations. The vast majority, approximately 3,500, are flavours, which affect the taste of foods and are not specifically regulated. Other classes which are not specifically regulated at present are enzymes (which speed up or help control chemical reactions), modified starches (which act as thickeners), and a range of chemicals used to help in food processing, such as encapsulating agents, whipping aids and crystallisation inhibitors.

About 330 individual additives are specifically permitted and regulated by the Government, either for general use in food, or for use in limited amounts in specific products. The main groups are colouring agents, emulsifiers, stabilisers and thickeners, preservatives, antioxidants, flavour enhancers and artificial sweeteners. Other categories include anti-caking agents, which prevent lumps forming in salt and powdery foods; additives to propel the contents out of spray containers; glazing agents to give a sheen to the surface of food; bleaching agents to whiten flour; substances to add bulk without calories in slimming foods; humectants to prevent food drying out; and additives to achieve a host of other functions covered in later chapters.

In general, food additives are used for three main purposes:

- to preserve food and prevent the growth of harmful organisms such as bacteria, thereby improving the keeping quality and hence the safety of food. This is their most useful function since bacteria and moulds can produce dangerous and potentially lethal toxins such as those which cause food poisoning
- to modify the consistency and texture of processed products such as soups, desserts, cakes and cooked meats, which affect the way food feels in your mouth ('mouth feel')
- to add colour or flavour to many foods, from squashes and yoghurts to cheese and pickles. This affects our sensory perception and appreciation.

There is also a category of substances called processing aids – these are used to stop ingredients sticking to machinery (as in confectionery manufacture); prevent foaming when boiling liquids or filling bottles; improve the way powders flow; remove caffeine in tea or coffee, for example. Processing aids are said to be additives only if they perform a function and are present in the final product – often processing aids almost disappear during manufacture, even though they may have an effect on the texture, for example, of the final product (see Chapter 3 for more on this). Only when a processing aid acts as an additive does it need to appear on the label.

Additives may also contribute essential nutrients, particularly vitamins, but when they are used solely for their vitamin or mineral properties, for example in cereals or baby foods, they may be classified as ingredients.

And the abuses . . .

Additives may increase the opportunities for debasing products, for example by increasing the quantity of water which the food can absorb. This practice is particularly prevalent in the processing of cooked meats and frozen fish. Manufacturers claim that consumers prefer 'more succulent' hams and chickens, so they sell products containing polyphosphates and added water. However, many retailers do now sell fresh and frozen chickens and cooked meats without polyphosphates.

In some cases additives are used to mask inferior ingredients, such as adding colour to sausages or cooked meats to disguise the use of rusk, bone and offal; or colouring products to suggest either that they contain fruit or that more fruit has been used than is the case. The use of red colouring in place of tomato, or cheese flavour instead of cheese may also mislead consumers as to quality, and can form unfair competition with higher quality, higher priced, products. Thickeners and gelling agents may make a product such as fruit pie filling appear to have a higher fruit content than it does, and can lead to or mask the use of lower quality ingredients than might be desirable.

Without any declaration of the proportions of ingredients used, it is virtually impossible for people to compare the quality of different varieties without buying them and doing their own comparative tests. Without adequate information on quality it is impossible to judge whether a product is a nutritious, low-price alternative, or merely a poor-quality substitute. Additives should never be used to deceive the consumer or to disguise faults, or spoilage, resulting from less wholesome or defective ingredients or bad manufacturing practice.

Some nutritionists also argue that additives may be used to reduce the nutritional value of food, or to make food of limited nutritional value appear appetising. Emulsifiers and stabilisers may disguise large quantities of fat, sugar and starch, while colours and flavours disguise the fact that the basic ingredients of very different foods, for example, instant soups and desserts, can be the same.

Defining need

When looking at the question of need for an additive, different people may have different opinions on what is necessary. Consumers have different and varying needs from manufacturers. Manufacturers need to minimise cost, retain their competitiveness, innovate and try to expand their market share in a static market. Together with retailers, they will try to provide a variety of products at a range of prices to meet the demands of different consumers. Manufacturers may say they need particular types of additives for certain purposes, but do consumers want the product if it is made in that way? Could the food be made without the additives? Would it restrict choice, or increase the cost? Even if the food is not of the highest quality, is it nutritious? Is it desirable to increase choice? Any assessment of need should take account of a variety of such questions, as well as the need for whom, in what, and for what purpose.

The Food Advisory Committee (FAC)* has drawn up a list of factors which it considers contribute to a case of need:

- the need to maintain the wholesomeness of food products up to the time they are consumed
- the need for food to be presented in a palatable and attractive manner

- convenience in purchasing, packaging, storage, preparation and use
- extension of dietary choice
- the need for nutritional supplementation
- any economic advantage.

In addition, the Committee requires that the nutritional value of food must not be adversely affected by the use of the additive; the additive must meet an appropriate specification of purity; the amount of the additive used should be restricted to the minimum necessary; the presence of the additive in a food should be declared to the consumer so that he or she is not misled about the nature, substance or quality of the food; and that the additive must be safe.

Consumers' needs

A balanced and nutritious diet

The overriding need for consumers is to be able to obtain a nutritious and balanced diet, at prices they can afford, throughout the year. As the FAC recognised in 1979, 'Consumers now expect to have available to them all the year round and at an economic price, foods which otherwise would be available only during short periods of the year. If all these desirable objectives are to be achieved, it is inevitable that an increasing proportion of the food supply must be subjected to some form of processing before it reaches the final consumer.' Implicit in the FAC's approach was that additives go hand in hand with processing, a feature that is increasingly being questioned by consumers.

*Before 1984, advice to Ministers on the use of additives which could be permitted for use in food was given by the Food Additives and Contaminants Committee, and on food quality and standards by the Food Standards Committee. In 1984, a new Food Advisory Committee (FAC) was established to carry out the functions of the previous two bodies. For ease of reading, and simplicity, these advisory committees are referred to throughout as the FAC. (See later in this Chapter and the Appendix for more information about the Committee's work.)

UNDERSTANDING ADDITIVES

Choice and variety – cosmetic additives

Most people in the UK demand a varied, enjoyable and attractive diet. Although consumers are conscious of the need for a healthy diet, surveys have shown that their main concern is to have convenience foods to suit the family's everyday requirements.

The vast majority of additives in use are not intended to protect public health, and may be considered cosmetic. They affect the taste, texture and appearance of foods, and arguably none of them are essential, in the sense that we can live without them, and will not become ill if they are not present. They contribute to the variety of food, and hence to people's enjoyment. It should be a matter of choice whether or not to consume them in the quantities in which they are now used.

Some modern foods could not exist without additives. Salad cream would separate (like some French dressings) if emulsifiers and stabilisers were not used. Margarine requires emulsifiers and stabilisers, and had it not been coloured yellow like butter, it is questionable whether it would have been as popular as it is now. Many instant desserts, packet soups and coffee creamers have complex combinations of additives to create their different characteristics. Spray cream requires a propellant to eject it from the can, while in the snack food and processed meat product areas additives have played a substantial part in changing staple foods into a wide variety of crisps, potato products, pâtés, sausages and sliced cured meats, with different compositions and flavours.

Most critical attention has been given to the need for colours. Technically, they could be removed altogether, and indeed one company has already done this in the case of a glucose drink, previously bright orange, which now looks like mineral water. Without added colour, many products such as squashes, canned fruit and iced lollies would be very pale, while jellies, sweets and instant desserts would almost cease to exist as we know them.

Retailers and manufacturers hold different views about the need for added colour, for example in tinned peas and strawberry products. Some claim success in removing the colour, and are marketing 'brown' strawberries and 'beige' canned peas as in

France. Their competitors say that these products are not commercially viable, and that the majority of customers prefer brightly coloured food. Any definition of need must take account of people's acceptance of products: aesthetic appeal is important.

The European Commission's Scientific Committee for Food (SCF – see Appendix) noted that 'Customs and traditions determine the expectations of the consumer, and food which does not have the appearance and texture within the normal range of variation to which the consumer is accustomed will be rejected.' It thought that there was a psychological need for colours and flavours in some foods. This view has been endorsed by retailers who have found, for example, that they could not sell meat products such as gala pie without added colour, since such foods turned unacceptably brown on exposure to the air. The FAC also concluded that since colour plays a significant part in our enjoyment of food, it should continue to be permitted.

The main difficulty in defining the needs of consumers is in trying to distinguish between the absolute technical necessity for additives to be used if certain products are to be produced at all, and people's desire for different foods, tastes and flavours. Some people, particularly children, like brightly coloured or highly flavoured products, and certainly demand novel foods, but they do not need them to provide an adequate and nutritious diet.

To provide the choice and variety demanded, it can be argued that some foods need at least certain additives. For others, the need may depend on the form in which the food is to be supplied, or the type of consumer for whom the product is intended. To make valid decisions, manufacturers and policy-makers have to find out what people want to eat, and whether they want additives to be included in new products, or to be used with more restraint.

Babies and children
Babies and infants do not require additives to meet their nutritional needs any more than adults do. The digestive systems of babies and young children are not fully developed, so additives used in baby foods are limited, and some additives are banned

by law. However, many baby foods include modified starches, thickeners which affect the texture of the food.

What are the alternatives? Is there a genuine need for the use of modified starches rather than the starches present in unprocessed foods, or available as foods themselves? As long as additives are harmless to the child, does it matter whether they are used to benefit the babies, or to help busy mothers with a convenient product? Are there other ways of achieving the same end?

For at least the first five years children's diets substantially depend on the foods chosen by parents, and from the age of one increasingly resemble adult diets. The use of convenience foods for children, and the presence of additives in a wide range of snacks, soft drinks, desserts, meats and some yoghurts, make it almost inevitable that children will consume substantial quantities of additives each year. In considering the needs of consumers, therefore, account should be taken of the fact that such foods are likely to be eaten by children, so must be safe for all ages.

Consumers with special needs

Consumers are not a homogeneous group and definitions of 'need' must also take account of that. For instance, vegetarians will take a different view of the need for additives derived from animal sources than the population in general. People with health problems also have particular requirements. Hence, in considering the need to expand the range of permitted artificial sweeteners, for example, the FAC emphasised the medical concern about obesity, the high consumption of sugar in Britain, and the potential for reducing tooth decay by introducing a range of sweeteners which were less likely to cause dental decay than sucrose.

The FAC also took the view that there was a need for bulking aids for use in special foods for people trying to slim, to increase bulk without calories; polydextrose (no number) and alpha-cellulose – E460(ii) – are permitted for this purpose. (The value of such foods in achieving long-term weight reduction has yet to be conclusively demonstrated.)

Sweeteners which require less insulin to digest them than an equivalent amount of sucrose enable diabetics to eat foods such as jams and confectionery which they would otherwise not be able to enjoy freely. In France and Belgium, such sweeteners are available only through chemists, not from food shops. However, if there is no risk to the population as a whole from consuming foods prepared for people with a specific medical condition, there seems little reason to restrict their sale.

Additives with a preservative effect

A distinction should be drawn between those additives which can be used to protect public health and those which are cosmetic. Preservatives inhibit the natural process of decay by slowing down the growth of yeasts, moulds and bacteria, reduce the likelihood of food poisoning, and extend the shelf-life of products. Antioxidants retard the process by which oils and fats become rancid, leading to the development of 'off' flavours. Deterioration of food can give rise to the development of toxic substances, so the use of some preservatives and antioxidants, or turning to an alternative form of processing, is both necessary and desirable. This is particularly true for meat products, and where the signs of deterioration, such as mould on cheese, or fermentation in squashes, may not be obvious and where the health risk is greater than most retailers and consumers are willing to accept.

Without these additives, some products would have to be bought daily and in much smaller quantities. There would be a higher rate of spoilage and waste. This appears to have been the case with the removal of preservatives in bread, which has reduced shelf-life from five to two days.

The need for preservatives, therefore, depends on the availability of alternatives to additives, and on the price that consumers are willing to pay in terms of time as well as money. Fruit-based squashes, for example, require preservatives because people use them over a long period, opening and closing the bottles during use, exposing them to warm conditions, particularly during the summer, thereby providing an ideal sweet environment in which bacteria can grow and yeasts ferment. High-juice squashes are now being sold without added preservatives, but they have a very short shelf-life compared with traditional squash. People are advised to keep them in the fridge and consume them within three weeks. Alternatively, diluted fruit drinks in sterile cartons are available but are more expensive than concentrated squash, and must also be kept in the fridge and used quickly. Most frozen and canned fruit and vegetables do not require preservatives, but meat products, even when frozen, often contain them because of concerns about the safety of the food in the domestic kitchen when it is being stored or thawed, particularly if the product is only going to be heated and not recooked. Preservatives may also be used to keep the food safe in the factory before it is frozen.

Preservatives and antioxidants are among the most strictly regulated additives in the UK, with limits in many cases on both the quantities permitted and the range of foods in which they can be used. It has been estimated that they account for only 1 per cent of all the additives in food, and are the least open to question on grounds of need.

Despite this, there is evidence of manufacturers' need taking precedence over consumers' need. For example, in the widely publicised examples of removing preservatives from yoghurt, and antioxidants from crisps and snacks, it was found that the additives did not perform any function in the final product which could not be achieved in some other way. The preservative in fruit yoghurt protected the fruit before it was added. Improved quality control, limiting the length of time that the fruit is held in the factory before use, controlling the packaging of the ingredients, and refrigerated distribution have removed the technical need, so it suited the manufacturers to withdraw the preservative. In the case of crisps, antioxidants were used to prevent the frying oil becoming rancid during processing. Most oils contain natural antioxidants but these are destroyed by heat. By improving the quality of the oils, controlling its storage and use, and limiting the crisps' shelf-life, antioxidants could be removed.

Price and quality factors

While choice and variety are important elements in consumers' definition of need, people are not always given sufficient information to know whether the use of an additive will affect the price and quality of a particular product.

Trading standards officers have found, for example, that the sausages with the lowest meat content are not necessarily the cheapest, but the use of colour can make them appear to have a high meat content. This is an important issue for those on a low income who may end up paying more for lower quality goods. If reductions in the cost of ingredients are passed on to consumers, and they are aware of what ingredients have been used, then it is up to them whether or not to buy the food. But this is not always the case. At present, the food labelling regulations are not specific enough to permit consumers to make that choice (see Chapter 3).

Indeed, relationships between price and the use of additives are not straightforward. Additive-free varieties may be more or less expensive than competing brands depending on the cost of ingredients and processing, and on levels of demand. While you might think that the removal of an additive would allow prices to fall, or even to remain constant, in practice if synthetic additives are replaced with natural alternatives or added ingredients, this can increase costs: although colour extracted from plant sources can be cheaper than synthetic colours, natural additives have to be used in much greater quantities to achieve what is considered to be a satisfactory result.

Provided that people know the contents of what they are buying and are able to make a fair comparison between products, the availability of a wide selection of products of differing quality and price ranges is beneficial, particularly to those on low incomes. At the moment, however, it isn't always clear what you are buying.

Quantities used

The question of how much of an additive is needed for a product to be of acceptable quality is also debatable, and in the past has largely been determined by consumer trials. People's choices might be influenced, however, if they were given information about additive content and quality before the trial, and were asked about the options – would people choose a product with a stronger lemon taste given by a lemon flavouring or a weaker one in which the 'lemoniness' came from real lemons?

People's tastes in the countries of the EEC differ; national regulations reflect this, so the amounts of additives which may be used vary. But if food is to be traded freely between countries and consumers are to be protected against widespread or excessive use of a particular additive, the EEC has said that the conditions for its use have to be specified on a Community basis. In other words, what is considered as acceptable by and for consumers in one country in the Community may have to be accepted by the others. Not surprisingly some EEC members have questioned this.

There is scope for limiting the quantity and range of additives used, as has happened with the widespread removal of colours from yoghurts, fish fingers, ice-creams and some sauces, products especially eaten by children. The shift to natural colours has also resulted in a lessening of the intensity of colour in drinks, and some canned foods but does not appear to have reduced demand for or enjoyment of these products. While many suppliers have taken the change in attitude to colours and flavours into account, this is by no means a unanimous approach on the part of industry.

In conclusion, consumers have two types of need for additives:

- that food is preserved to protect it against bacterial contamination and the presence of toxins
- that their demand for choice and variety is satisfied.

There is little doubt about the importance of some additives for food preservation, but it is not possible to make categorical statements about the use of other additives to increase choice: it is often a matter of personal preference. Choice is effective only when it is informed, however. People's attitudes are changing as they gain information about developments in the food industry. They are beginning to ask whether it is misleading to market carbonated water with added colours and flavours to make a variety of different soft drinks. Is raspberry flavour yoghurt coloured pink a deception when there are no raspberries in the product at all? They want to know what additives are being used for in order to express an opinion on whether they are necessary.

Manufacturers' needs

Manufacturers claim two sorts of need for food additives – technical and economic.

Technical need

For the vast majority of additives, need is determined by the food chemists and manufacturers, who identify a use for a particular additive and market it accordingly. For additives governed by permitted lists, however, they must first seek approval for a new additive, and demonstrate a clear technical advantage in using the substance. The additive then has to be cleared for safety. Once permitted for a particular purpose, most additives, with the exception of certain preservatives, antioxidants, mineral hydro-carbons and those which are prohibited in baby foods, may be used in any foods for any purpose.

The main limits on the use of permitted additives are therefore the technical limitations imposed by the additives themselves, good manufacturing practice and the ingenuity of the food technologists.

To provide reliable quality The technical need for many additives has been well documented by manufacturers making individual cases to the FAC. For example, natural starches thicken foods, such as sauces, gravies and convenience products; they can improve the texture and appearance of puddings, and allow the consistency to be controlled during processing; they may slow down or prevent the separation of oils and fats in salad dressings, and prevent caking in foods such as icing sugar. Natural starches, however, do not perform well if cooked for long periods, at high temperatures, or when thawed after freezing. By modifying these starches with chemicals, many of these technological problems can be overcome. Modified starches are permitted for this reason.

UNDERSTANDING ADDITIVES

People have come to expect standardised products that do not vary from batch to batch. The use of additives enables products to be made to precise specifications of colour, texture and flavour, which are not affected by seasonal variations in supply or fluctuations in quality. For example, in beer- and wine-making the quality of the raw materials can vary substantially according to the weather, but additives may be used to offset any variations.

Additives may also replace features such as colour, flavour or vitamins that are otherwise lost in processing. Vitamin C in oranges, for example, is destroyed in the production of squash. Ascorbic acid (E300) is used to replace the vitamin, and may also function as an antioxidant to stop the flavour deteriorating.

To achieve particular effects Some additives have specialised uses. Without emulsifiers, fat would float on the surface of ice-cream and margarine would separate. Flour improvers make bread and cakes lighter. Nitrites and nitrates are essential for the traditional colour and flavour of bacon and cured meats, as well as acting as preservatives.

In some products two additives may meet technical need better than one, for example where one additive increases the effect of the other.

Where additives perform better than other alternatives Artificial colours and flavours have technical advantages over natural sources in some products. Firstly, the colour or flavour is more intense and does not undergo seasonal variation. Artificial flavours also offer a wider range of tastes than natural alternatives.

Some natural colours are highly sensitive to light and fade during storage, for example in squashes in clear glass bottles, or in products in transparent packaging. Nor will natural colours tolerate the very high temperatures used in some manufacturing processes. Suppliers keen to remove artificial colours from their products have had particular problems in trying to replace erythrosine (E127), for example, in cherry products. Erythrosine is currently the only permitted colour which resembles that of cherries and is also heat-stable. Without erythrosine, cherries would fade during processing, and in cakes might go brown, producing an unattractive and unsatisfactory product. Some manufacturers are now producing glacé cherries coloured with anthocyanins (E163) which make them darker but not unacceptable.

To ensure safety as well as an adequate shelf-life Most of the preservatives and antioxidants come within this category, in which the technical need and that of consumers overlap. Both types of additive perform functions which are essential to protect the health of consumers, and permit a shelf-life long enough for products to be commercially viable. While it is possible to remove additives, the alternative may sometimes result in a different product with significantly different characteristics from the original because it has to be stored more carefully, or the different processing technique radically changes the product.

Preservation using additives is not the only means available. With faster distribution, better temperature control throughout the food chain, and rapid turnover, the large retailers who dominate the market with about 75 per cent of trade have been able to reduce the shelf-life of products, and reduce the need for preservatives. This option is not open to small retailers and corner shops who do not have the same turnover or degree of control over the distribution.

To enable certain manufacturing processes to be performed Technical need may depend on the processing methods used. For example, encapsulants are required to convert liquids such as flavours or essential oils into free-flowing fine powders for use in dry mixes. Solvents can separate a food into individual components, allowing flavour to be extracted, or contaminants removed.

Processing aids may be required to stop food sticking to machinery, or to control its flow, for example in chocolate-making. In many instances, however, the substances perform no function in the final product. The residues may be very small, but nevertheless may be found in some products.

Before an additive is approved, manufacturers must show that there is a technical benefit in using it, but that reason is not sufficient on its own. For example, although one enzyme, penicillinase, is able to remove residues of antibiotics from milk, the FAC did not accept that as sufficient reason for permitting its use, when the existing method of control – discarding the contaminated milk – was preferable to protect consumers.

Assessment of technical need should always take account of the alternative ways of achieving the same effect. Freezing or heat-treating fruit that is going into jam or yoghurt makes it less crucial to treat the raw materials with sulphites to kill yeasts and mould spores. If vegetables are canned at a sufficiently high temperature, they become sterile and do not need a preservative. Freezing, an effective means of extending shelf-life and preserving products, removes the need for some additives (although in some cases preservatives are added in order to protect the customer while the product is being defrosted). However, all of these options may increase production costs and hence prices.

While the use of synthetic colouring agents has been widespread because they are more reliable than natural colours, have a more intense colour, and are more stable in use, added colour is not essential: technically it is possible to sell a range, if more limited, of attractive, wholesome and nutritious foods without added colour, albeit with paler and inconsistent colours. Squashes with a high juice content, or yoghurts with 30 per cent fruit, do not need added colour because there is enough colour in the fruit.

Technical need is therefore largely a question of alternatives. However, manufacturers may sometimes justify the use of additives as a substitute for more expensive processes and ingredients: using antioxidants is cheaper than freezing or vacuum-packing; emulsifiers allow more extensive use of oils and fats so that the apparent quality of the product is maintained without using as much of the ingredients; polyphosphates increase the quantity of water that can be retained in meat, and hence add to the weight with sometimes only a marginal increase in processing cost.

Economic need
The food industry today is highly competitive, and trying to retain profitability in the face of changing markets is difficult. In

Western Europe the total food market is stagnant. There is a finite quantity of food which people can eat. Food manufacturers try to increase their market share by introducing new products or new varieties, and increasing their profits. The production of a wide variety of crisps and yoghurts from two much cheaper products, potatoes and milk, are examples of doing this successfully. Convenience foods, TV dinners and gourmet meals have all recently demonstrated that consumers are willing to pay high prices for labour-saving products. Additives have contributed to the range of products which the food industry can produce.

Food manufacturers use more than 200,000 tonnes of additives a year in the UK, with a 1984 market value of as much as £231 million. This has evident advantages for employment, for profits in the chemical industries, and in aiding innovation in food processing.

The economic factors which influence manufacturers and retailers vary. For instance, one manufacturer of meat products informed us that while all new products developed for retail sale should be able to bear the claim 'Free from all artificial colours and flavours', in the case of the brand used in the catering sector 'we make no such restrictions, as the cost factor plays a major role in this area and thus we make use of any additive (providing it is permitted in the UK) as required for product safety and quality.'

One of the few occasions when the FAC has recorded views on economic need was in considering the request for the antioxidants BHA and BHT to be allowed in chewing-gum base. The initial request was refused on the grounds that they were not needed. It was subsequently noted that natural antioxidants were destroyed during the purification process. The inability to replace these limited the life of the gum bases to three months, but since the base was imported by sea, the need to speed distribution increased costs to the industry, gave insufficient time to cope with shipping delays, and put UK manufacturers at a disadvantage with American, Canadian, Australian and New Zealand competitors. The addition of the antioxidant, it was claimed, doubled the shelf-life and led to a better quality product. The arguments were accepted and the antioxidant's use permitted, although doubts about safety remain, and although consumption of chewing-gum can hardly be considered essential either in economic or nutritional terms.

In recent years the removal of an additive from a product has often occurred as a result of pressure from consumers to discontinue its use, perhaps on grounds of health, rather than because it has been banned or because there has been a potential marketing advantage to be gained from making the change. Although removing an additive may reduce the cost of the ingredients, the relationship between the price of the final product and the saving can rarely be identified. Economic benefits which may accrue to manufacturers are not easily identifiable without detailed information about production and distribution costs.

There are many considerations which will determine the price the consumer pays for a product. Where the removal of an additive has reduced the shelf-life of a product, as in the case of bread, some retailers will reduce the quantities they purchase in order to minimise wastage. Retailers may price the new product competitively with the old, or with other competitors. Changes to product specifications may have taken place as part of a comprehensive review of all ingredients, not just of the additives. None of the retailers we spoke to could give a clear answer about the effect of removing additives on price, but pointed out that in any case costs could increase where one type of additive was being substituted for another, or where the additive's removal involved increasing the number, amount or quality of other ingredients. The economic implications for consumers have been paid little attention.

Who decides what's needed?

The Food Advisory Committee

The Food Act 1984 obliges Ministers to restrict, as far as is practicable, the use of substances of no nutritional value as foods or ingredients. Ministers take advice from the Food Advisory Committee (FAC), and before any new additive in the regulated groups can be approved for use in the UK, manufacturers must convince the FAC that there is a need for it. (For further details, see the Appendix.)

The main influences on the FAC's assessment of need come from the suppliers of the additive and the food manufacturers seeking approval to use a new additive. The FAC requires them to submit evidence that the additive performs a new function in food or, better, performs an existing function, with clear benefits to the consumer. The case must be supported by full details of the substance, toxicological data, and the results from any trials in which it has been used in food. It must also have substantial support among manufacturers.

There are two weaknesses in this approach. Firstly, the FAC bases its assessments not on independent research, but on information supplied to it by manufacturers. It is generally only when the Committee has made a recommendation, and draft proposals are circulated for comment, that consumer organisations get an opportunity to comment, although the FAC has a few members with a consumer background. Even then, they are unlikely to have the resources to evaluate individual additives. No consumer groups made representations to the FAC during the review (published in 1987) of the regulations on colouring matter in food although they have commented subsequently on the recommendations.

Secondly, while the FAC compares the potential advantages of using a new additive against alternative processing methods, it is mainly dependent on manufacturers' views. A manufacturer wishing to gain approval for a new additive cannot be relied upon to provide an objective assessment of whether the proposed new additive can bring about the desired effect better than existing alternatives. In permitting the use of a new additive, consideration is given to whether others, which previously performed a similar function, are still needed or can be removed from the list. But without the ability to commission research, the FAC is limited in the extent to which it can judge alternatives, although it can call upon MAFF's resources.

The FAC acknowledged in its 1987 report on colours that 'the views of society have changed' and that 'the purchaser of processed foods is more aware of the use of additives and is increasingly calling into question their use'. This should require it to be more stringent in the future than in the past in assessing need, and in reviewing the continuing need for some additives already in use. On the whole, however, it is able only to review additive groups when requested by Ministers.

Technical need changes over time: at the start of the twentieth century, preservatives in milk were considered essential to meet the nation's requirements. The introduction of refrigeration and motorised distribution removed that need, and British consumers have become accustomed to preservative-free milk – indeed, preservatives are no longer permitted in milk. There are other foods for which the availability of refrigeration has reduced or removed the need for preservatives, as in yoghurts, and more changes may be possible.

The speed with which antioxidants have been removed from crisps and snacks has led people to question whether they were ever needed. However, at the time when they were introduced, when demand was lower, distribution slower, and the manufacturing processes less sophisticated, antioxidants would have contributed to the shelf-life, and helped the crisps retain their quality over time. Manufacturers now cook in higher-quality oils, control the processing conditions better and use light-proof packaging so that the antioxidants are no longer necessary. Since technical need changes, it should be re-evaluated more frequently by the FAC.

Manufacturers

Once an additive appears on a permitted list (with the exception of preservatives and antioxidants), it may be used in most foodstuffs. Many other additives (including flavours, enzymes and certain processing aids) are not specifically regulated, so in practice it is the manufacturers and food technologists who really decide what they will use and for which purposes.

Many manufacturers, and retailers purchasing own-brand goods, have policies on the use of additives in their products. These range from those who choose to limit severely the use of additives, to those who consider it reasonable to use any additives from the permitted lists as well as other unregulated additives, provided they meet the requirements of the Food Act and its implementing Regulations. Several manufacturers told us that the philosophy of their company was to avoid using additives wherever possible; in one company, board approval was required for each additive used.

A few manufacturers, such as those producing cereals, made statements on the lines that 'additives would be used only where they would impart some benefit to the product', but what they actually mean is unclear since they include colours and flavours as well as vitamins in their definition of beneficial substances. A confectionery manufacturer commented: 'Defining the need for an additive is a purely practical matter: can the product be made without it, is the product's consumer appeal significantly improved by it?' Another said: 'We recognise that the colour, flavour and texture of food are important attributes in determining the palatability and acceptability of the product to the consumer.' Some companies which do not use additives nevertheless turn a blind eye to additives which may be in the ingredients themselves.

A company well known for its beer told us: 'Additives and processing aids shall be used only where there is a proven technical need, where they are harmless to the consumer and where their use is of ultimate benefit to the consumer. The principles of company policy on this subject are based on protection of health, avoidance of consumer exploitation and on good standards of manufacturing practice.'

The ways manufacturers interpret their policies vary, but there are common themes. None would remove an additive if it were likely to jeopardise the safety of the product in any way. In several instances, however, a reduction in shelf-life has been accepted by manufacturers (although in the case of bread, not without resistance from the public). As one soft drink manufacturer expressed it: 'Where we have changed additives we have thoroughly evaluated them first. Generally, shelf-life has been adversely affected but still remains within acceptable limits for us. Had shelf-life been too seriously affected, then the change in additives would not have been contemplated.'

Most manufacturers will not accept any deterioration in quality, which is sometimes interpreted to mean 'will not accept any change in the appearance, palatability, or stability', while for others change is possible provided that it is acceptable to consumers. Changes in flavour and in the shade and stability of colour come into this category.

The policies of removing additives are almost entirely in response to perceptions of consumer need. 'We do produce some products with fewer artificial additives. This is purely for marketing purposes. We do not believe that products containing artificial additives are any less healthy or any less safe.' Manufacturers and retailers are in a better position, however, to assess consumers' preference for a product containing certain additives, once that additive is in use, than at the time when they are making submissions for a new additive.

Retailers particularly acknowledge that there are cases where additives have been used in products where they were not technically needed, and of no benefit to consumers. This occurred, for example, in the addition of colours to crisps. There was no justifiable need, so these have now been removed.

A more stringent approach?

The additives issue has shown how consumers can demonstrate their power to influence the supply and range of food available, and to make clear their views on additive use. If people are not willing to consume a particular substance in their food, then the question of whether or not it is necessary becomes irrelevant.

Retailers and manufacturers have responded to people's desire to reduce the number of additives in food. The assumption, however, that because some additives can be removed, there is no need for any, is erroneous. Need is a rather intangible concept, and will differ according to who defines it and for whom the product is intended. There is an inherent difference in considering need between those additives which have a preservative function and which contribute to food safety, and those which are purely cosmetic. Texture modifiers such as emulsifiers, stabilisers, thickeners and gelling agents form an intermediate group which have avoided widespread scrutiny. For the cosmetic additives, and the texture modifiers, need becomes much more a question of what consumers want, look for and can afford than the technical functions performed. The definition of need should put advantage to consumers first. A food additive should not be permitted unless there is a positive advantage for consumers from its use and where its use serves a purpose which cannot be achieved by other economically or technologically practicable means.

The rapid growth in the use of food additives during the past twenty years highlights some of the weaknesses inherent in the way the concept of need has been applied, and in particular:

- the failure to ask consumers what uses they consider to be justifiable, such as in taste tests
- the failure to review regularly the need for all the additives in use
- the failure to limit the range of foods and the quantities in which most additives can be used.

Once permitted, additives have been reviewed infrequently, and such reviews have concentrated on those additives for which additional safety data has been requested, and not on those which were once needed but are no longer necessary. Indeed, comprehensive reviews of a whole class of additives, such as the one on colours, are rare (and that took about ten years to achieve). The report indicates that the FAC will apply stricter criteria to need in the future. It proposes limits on the quantities of colouring which may be added to food, and also to prohibit the use of colours in foods which until now have not contained colour. The impact of such reviews is wholly dependent on whether Ministers act on their recommendations, and in the past they have not always done so.

Even if the system for assessing the need for new additives is tightened up, there will remain substantial numbers of additives, mostly flavours, in use which are unregulated, the need for which has not been proven.

Need should be reassessed in the light of changing public opinion, and food manufacturers should perhaps be required to prove consumers' approval as well as technical need before applying for proposed new uses.

UNDERSTANDING ADDITIVES

The FAC must be convinced that there is a genuine need for the additive and that its use will not adversely affect the nutritional value of the food or consumers' health. It also considers whether the benefit can be achieved by an existing additive or any other means. However, while it recognises the need for food to be wholesome, palatable and attractive, it does not spell out the counter argument that additives should not be used to disguise inferior quality food or faulty processing or to deceive the customer. As subsequent chapters show, there is evidence that additives have indeed been used in this way: the limited control on the foods in which additives may be used, and the absence of regular review of those permitted, has led to abuse.

2
Can additives damage your health?

Many people are concerned that additives may be damaging their health. Their worries have been fuelled by press reports of additives causing adverse reactions or being associated with the development of cancers. Claims that children's health is at risk from the range and quantity of additives they eat have also been made. What has been the basis for these concerns? Are they justified?

According to MAFF, 'the general medical view is that additives are safe and do not harm health – for most people. There are a very few people who have a reaction to additives . . . just as there are a few people who are allergic to foods such as strawberries or shellfish. In fact, more people are allergic to natural substances than to man-made additives.'*

An EEC official responsible for food standards has also said that food additives are basically safe, and because they are subjected to rigorous safety testing, they may be safer than some unprocessed foods. So why are people concerned?

There is no such thing as an absolute guarantee of safety. As many scientists have pointed out, all foods and food ingredients are potentially toxic if consumed at very high levels. Humans cannot live without certain essential nutrients such as zinc, copper and vitamin A, but in excess these are very toxic. Many natural foods such as peanuts, red kidney beans, mushrooms and fruit juices contain small amounts of toxic substances. Dr David Richardson (Fellow of the Institute of Food Science and Technology, and of the Royal Society of Medicine, and head of

Food additives: the balanced approach (published by MAFF, 1987).

laboratory and scientific services for the Nestlé Company) claimed in 1987 that 'current scientific knowledge indicates that no food, even if it contains an intrinsically toxic component either present naturally or added as an intentional additive, poses a hazard to human health and well-being *when taken in moderation and as part of a nutritionally balanced diet*' (author's italics).

The risks to health from food additives pale into insignificance when compared with the risks of developing heart disease or bowel cancer, both of which have been associated with aspects of diet. A study carried out in 1983 looked at all the estimates of the risk of death from cancer caused by one of a variety of environmental causes. The estimates of the risks associated with diet ranged from 10 to 70 per cent of all cancer deaths, those with food additives from 0 to 2 per cent.

Nevertheless, that is no reason for exposing people to risk from specific additives or for failing to ensure that the highest levels of safety assessment are maintained. And risks that are acceptable for products which are vital to sustain life may be unacceptable for less essential food products or where additives could be avoided altogether.

What is safe?

Substances which do not adversely affect our health
In the UK it is an offence to add any substance to food or use any ingredient which 'renders the food injurious to health'. In determining whether a particular food is injurious to health, the Food Act 1984 permits account to be taken both of the probable immediate effect, and the probable cumulative effect, on people eating the food 'in ordinary quantities'. Ministers have power to 'require, prohibit or regulate' the addition of any substance to food. Additives which appear on permitted lists are specifically regulated; both need and safety are evaluated before permission is granted for their use. When legislators assure us that additives are 'safe', they draw on this definition.

All other additives must conform to the general requirement that food should not harm public health. This is a very general requirement, essentially leaving it to the courts to decide whether a substance can be deemed to have 'damaged public health'. As far as is known, no one in the UK has died from consuming additives. It remains a matter of contention whether the fact that some people suffer adverse reactions from particular additives is considered to be 'injurious to health', and so far whether an adverse reaction from a food additive counts as being harmful to health has not been tested in the courts. Since most of the additives known to be implicated in adverse reactions are specifically permitted by regulations, such an action would be unlikely to succeed.

Level of intake

'Safety' is defined in the USA as 'a reasonable certainty that a substance is not harmful under the intended conditions of use'. For the SCF (see the Appendix) the definition is 'socially acceptable potential risk' under the existing or predicted conditions of consumption or exposure. The potential harm from a substance depends on how much of it somebody consumes. There are therefore two parts to any safety assessment: first, whether the substance itself exhibits any toxic properties in experimental conditions; second, the likely level of intake, which depends on the amount of the additive likely to be used, the foods to which it may be added, and the part these foods play in the average diet. All need to be assessed before a decision on safety can be made.

A joint international committee of expert toxicologists (JECFA – see the Appendix for further details) meets annually under the auspices of the United Nations World Health and Food and Agriculture Organisations to consider the general principles governing the use of food additives, which includes safety. The committee reviews whether or not substances have toxic effects by looking at evidence from animal experiments which could have implications for humans. On the basis of their assessment, it recommends maximum Acceptable Daily Intakes (ADIs). These are defined as 'the daily dose of a chemical that will be without appreciable risk (to humans) on the basis of all the known facts at the time'. ADIs are established in milligrams per kilogram of body weight and represent the estimated amount that can be consumed over a lifetime without damage to health. ADIs are generally used as a starting point for recommending maximum human intake.

The SCF may also set ADIs when asked by the European Commission to review the safety of particular additives. The levels set may differ from those of JECFA depending on the date of the assessment and the evidence available at the time.

Safety in the UK

Ultimately, in the UK the power to decide what may be added to food rests with the two Ministers of Health and of Agriculture, Fisheries and Food, who are jointly responsible for regulations limiting the use of additives. Recommendations are made to them by the FAC, which takes advice on the safety of proposed new additives – and any others Ministers ask it to review – from the Committee on the Toxicity of Chemicals in Food, Consumer Products and the Environment (COT – see Appendix). It may also take advice from the Committee on Medical Aspects of Food Policy, the Committee on Carcinogenicity of Chemicals in Food, Consumer Products and the Environment, and from the Committee on Mutagenicity of Chemicals in Food, Consumer Products and the Environment.

In assessing safety, the COT takes into account information on the chemical properties of the additive and the way it is manufactured. These are looked at alongside the results of experiments where animals are fed the additive, laboratory tests to show whether there are any effects on cells, and results from any human trials or experience. These scientific results are then considered in the light of the proposed uses in food and the amounts which people are likely to consume as a result. MAFF supplies estimates of the levels of consumption which are likely to arise from the uses proposed by the manufacturers. When a class of permitted additives is being more generally reviewed, MAFF may also carry out studies of people's diets to investigate how much of a group of additives is being consumed. When the risk to human health is considered acceptably low, the substance is said to be safe.

The COT has no facilities to carry out its own testing, but considers reports of relevant investigations carried out by or on behalf of the industry or the particular manufacturer concerned, research associations, international organisations and others. It also takes into account the views of the international scientific community, and reports written by scientists worldwide, irrespective of whether they are formally submitted for consideration. The COT usually classifies the additives it considers into one of five groups:

Group 'A' Substances which the available evidence suggests are acceptable for use in food.

Group 'B' Substances which on the available evidence may be regarded as provisionally acceptable for use in food, but about which further information must be made available within a specified time.

Group 'C' Substances for which the available evidence suggests possible toxicity and which ought not to be permitted for use in food until adequate evidence of safety has been provided to establish their acceptability.

Group 'D' Substances for which the available information indicates definite or probable toxicity and which ought not to be permitted for use in food.

Group 'E' Substances for which inadequate or no toxicological data are available, so it is not possible to say whether they are acceptable for use in food.

Only substances from Groups 'A' and 'B' may be recommended for use as food additives. The COT has stated that neither a Group 'A' nor a Group 'B' classification is a guarantee of absolute safety. In the case of Group 'A' substances, the Committee is satisfied that there is sufficient toxicological information, of an acceptable standard, for it to conclude that the additive is likely to be free of any adverse effects in humans when consumed at the maximum levels which might arise from its use in food. Although no additional information is required, if new information suggests that there may be previously unrecognised or undetected adverse effects in animals or humans, or that advances in toxicology call for new tests to be carried out, the COT reviews the substance. The requirement that additives should be free from any adverse effects on humans appears stringent, but despite that some substances known to be toxic at high levels or which cause adverse reactions in some individuals have been given an 'A' classification.

The COT makes recommendations to the FAC about whether the additive may be used, and in some cases it suggests conditions governing the level of use, the foods for which it is acceptable or the purposes for which it is safe; it may also recommend as a matter of caution that use in foods for certain categories of people, such as children, or by those with particular medical conditions, should be restricted.

The relationship between decisions on safety and levels of use is clearly demonstrated in the FAC's 1987 report on colours, for example in the case of erythrosine (E127). Animal experiments had indicated increases in the thyroid weights of rats which may indicate that erythrosine can lead to cancers. Human studies suggested that effects on the thyroid might occur beyond a certain level. Although the COT considered that there was no risk from erythrosine at the levels in the average human diet, people who eat excessive amounts of food containing erythrosine, which is likely to include children, may have intakes approaching one-tenth to one-third of the level at which effects on the thyroid might occur. The COT felt that for an adequate safety margin limits should be set on the use of erythrosine in products such as glacé cherries, biscuits, confectionery and preserves.

The views of the COT normally have a major influence on the ultimate recommendation to Ministers from the FAC. However, in the case of erythrosine, the FAC recommended that it be permitted only in cocktail and glacé cherries, for which the case of need was greatest, but up to a level which the COT considered might start to have harmful effects. Meanwhile, unless or until Ministers act on the FAC recommendation, erythrosine continues to be used in unlimited quantities in jams, jam fillings for some sponges, cherry products such as cakes, tinned pie fillings, instant desserts, some cooked meats, chocolates and sweets.

In the UK, no additive appears on a permitted list without having gone through a detailed process of assessment and review. The safety assessments of some additives, however, were carried out some years ago and have not been recently reviewed in the light of changing use and patterns of consumption. There is very limited, if any, checking of levels of use. It is left to producers to follow 'good manufacturing practice' which means that the additive should be used at the minimum level necessary to achieve the desired effect; that it must not conceal adulteration of the food or the use of inferior quality ingredients; and that it must not create a nutritional imbalance.

Risks versus benefits

For some additives, particularly preservatives and antioxidants, scientists have had to weigh up the potential long-term risks from using those additives against known public health hazards, for example from food poisoning organisms. Botulism, a rare but lethal form of food poisoning, has been practically eliminated, because when foods are treated with nitrites and then heated, the spores that cause botulism are killed. If nitrite is not used, the spores can be destroyed only at very high temperatures, which will affect the product.

Some people would like to see nitrites banned because of evidence that they can form nitrosamines in the body. Nitrosamines are powerful carcinogens in animals (that is, they can cause cancers), and can also cause other abnormalities in human and animal cells. It has been accepted internationally that if certain cooked meats, bacon and sausages did not contain nitrites, they would present a substantial health hazard; manufacturers and retailers are unwilling to risk this in the absence of a satisfactory alternative.

Similarly difficult decisions have faced the COT in evaluating the safety of the antioxidants BHA and BHT, both of which exhibit toxic properties in animal experiments. In assessing the need for them to be used, against the worries over safety, the

COT has expressed concern about the lack of satisfactory alternatives to prevent the development of toxins in oils and fats which become rancid on exposure to air.

However, it is possible to find cooked meats, for example, that do not contain nitrites, and traditional sausages with a high meat content without preservative. Some manufacturers use vitamin E with a substance that will increase its antioxidant effect in place of BHA and BHT, or have removed the antioxidants altogether, where there is a natural antioxidant present in the food.

It is possible to limit the use of substances whose safety is in doubt, but there may be implications for manufacturing processes, as well as effects on shelf-life and costs to consumers. Like need, assessment of safety is a matter of judgement: it is not absolute.

The safety risks

Allergies and adverse reactions

The term 'allergy' is widely and somewhat inaccurately used to describe reactions to food additives. Adverse reactions to food and food additives can be more appropriately defined as:

Food intolerance – an unpleasant reaction to food which is not psychologically based and which occurs even when the food is disguised. This may include true allergies in which the body's immune system reacts with unpleasant effects to a small amount of a substance to which the person has previously been exposed.

Food aversion – an unpleasant reaction caused by emotions associated with a food, but which does not occur when the food is disguised.

Some people are known to suffer from adverse reactions to certain foodstuffs, and this can include reactions to additives. Debate rages about the extent of the problem. A MAFF report on priorities for food safety research noted that there was a lack of adequate information, but added 'media comment often assumes that food intolerance and food allergy, especially that induced by food additives, is much more common than can be deduced from the available evidence.'

The SCF estimated in 1982 that between 3 and 15 people in every 10,000 in the population may suffer reactions to food additives. MAFF estimates that for everyone who may have an adverse reaction to a food additive possibly as many as 30 or more may experience problems from foods such as milk, eggs, wheat or soya. Against this background, MAFF started a research programme in 1987 to study the incidence of adverse reactions in the general population, and the mechanisms which may be involved.

The SCF's estimate was corroborated by the results of the MAFF study: only in a very few cases do clinically reproducible symptoms occur as a result of the consumption of additives in the amounts likely to be present in food. As part of the study, ten per cent of the population in the Wycombe Health Authority in Buckinghamshire, 30,000 people, were sent a questionnaire designed to identify those who thought that they suffered adverse reactions to additives. Eighty-one people who stated that they had a problem took part in detailed medical screening. Participants were tested with a combination of colours, preservatives, antioxidants and aspirin. Of these 81, only three people showed positive reactions. Two had adverse reactions to annatto, and one to a cocktail of colours. This gives a percentage rate for the population of between 0.01 and 0.26 per cent, close to the lower level identified by the SCF. Put another way, however, Britain's population of 56 million could include between 5,500 and 112,000 people who potentially have adverse reactions to additives in foodstuffs.

It is now generally believed that the people who react to some additives also have adverse reactions to other foods or substances. For instance, people who experience an adverse reaction to aspirin seem more likely to react to certain additives. The mechanisms by which these effects occur is being studied.

Four groups of additives are under particular scrutiny: colours, antioxidants, preservatives and flavour enhancers. The colours which have been analysed in most detail are the azo dyes – tartrazine (E102) in particular – although the natural colour annatto (E160b) can also cause reactions. Among the preservatives, the benzoates (E210–E219) and sulphites (E220–E227) commonly found in squashes, drinks and fruit preserves are known to be implicated, as are the antioxidants BHA (E320) and BHT (E321).

Reactions range from minor skin complaints (dermatitis and rashes) to serious respiratory conditions, including asthma. A report on food intolerance and food aversion by the Royal College of Physicians and the British Nutrition Foundation commented that the most commonly reported manifestations of food intolerance associated with food additives are in the skin (usually nettlerash or swelling) and in the respiratory tract (particularly asthma and the production of excess catarrh). Migraine and bowel irritation have also been reported.

Irrespective of how widespread is the problem of adverse reactions to food additives, there is no doubt that for those who suffer it is a health hazard. Legislators have been faced with three options:

- to prohibit the additives in question. The Norwegian Government adopted this stance in 1978 by banning the use of artificial colours. No research has been conducted to see whether the incidence of eczema or asthma has fallen as a result. The Norwegians have not, however, banned the use of the preservatives that are associated with adverse reactions because they consider them to be essential in the absence of any completely satisfactory substitutes
- to restrict their use. This is how the Swedish Government reacted, and since 1980 azo dyes have been mainly limited to spirits, cocktail cherries and caviare
- to label them. The UK Government has chosen this approach on the basis that people who are at risk can scan labels and avoid substances to which they have an adverse reaction. It is not always possible for those at risk to avoid additives, however, because of the lack of comprehensive labelling (see Chapter 3). (A data bank was set up in 1987 at the Leatherhead Food Research Association, so that members of the medical profession and dietitians can find out which of

various brands of food are free from certain additives, but the information is not comprehensive since some manufacturers have not been so forthcoming.)

The official position in the UK is relaxed, and while more research is being encouraged there is scepticism in the Ministries concerned about the extent of the problem. The FAC recognises the real concern among the public, but accepts the COT's view that 'the occurrence of intolerance to food additives . . . is unlikely to be common'. In the United States, too, the Food and Drugs Administration advisory committee in 1986 concluded that tartrazine, benzoic acid and its sodium salt, aspartame and monosodium glutamate present no serious risks at current levels of usage.

The SCF's 1982 report recommended, however, that all additives should be labelled as a basic precaution: that there should be a restriction on the amount of colourings permitted in food, and that those additives such as colours with a purely aesthetic function but which provoke adverse reactions should not be permitted.

The debate about adverse reactions has raised questions about the extent to which children are at risk, and in particular whether additives are associated with hyperactivity. The Hyperactive Children's Support Group consider MAFF's figure that about 1 in 10,000 people suffer adverse reactions to be a gross underestimate in relation to children, but they do not have the resources to conduct a scientific survey of the extent of the problem.

Dr Ben Feingold (an American allergy specialist) highlighted the problem in the late 1960s, when he indicated that hyperactivity in some children could be reduced by progressively excluding artificial colours, flavours, preservatives, and BHA and BHT from the diet, while simultaneously cutting down on sugar consumption. Results of research published in the *Lancet* in 1985 showed that hyperactive children may experience reactions to a diet including artificial colours and preservatives, but each child was also sensitive to other substances. The Hyperactive Children's Support Group has also found that of the children referred to them by parents and doctors worried about overactivity, problems of control, bed-wetting and behavioural problems, about 79 per cent improve on a Feingold diet. Improvements in the performance of school children, and in the personality of prisoners in the United States as a result of changing the quality of the diet and reducing consumption of additives, have also been widely publicised.

Differences of view continue about whether 'hyperactivity' is a defineable medical condition and the extent to which behavioural problems are a response to environmental factors or diet. Very little satisfactory work has been done on hyperactivity and there is much disagreement among experts on what the term means, let alone its causes.

The fact is that we do not know whether children are at risk of developing hyperactivity from additives, or whether those with a medically confirmed condition of hyperactivity are more likely to experience adverse reactions to additives. Recent work at Guys and the Brompton Hospitals suggests that most adverse reactions to food in children occur during the first two years of their lives, but is not permanent – most grow out of it by the age of three. This underlines the problem of whether the safety margins for young children are sufficient.

Cancer

Substances which are known to cause cancer are called carcinogens. In the United States, the Delany Amendment to the Constitution requires that any potential carcinogen be banned. This view is supported by some toxicologists and consumer groups who believe that there is no level at which a carcinogen is safe. It is not a unanimous view, and others consider that an 'acceptably low' risk can be determined.

Evidence of carcinogenicity resulted in the widespread banning of cyclamates (see Chapter 6) in the late 1960s following reports of possible cancer of the bladder in rats fed cyclamate mixed with saccharin. None of the subsequent studies confirmed this effect, and it is now known that the bladder cancer was caused by the saccharin not the cyclamate. Yet saccharin is still permitted: while the COT accepted that saccharin is associated with increased bladder cancer in rats, the Committee decided that saccharin should be given Group 'B' status on the basis of studies of its effects on man. These studies 'failed to show an association between saccharin use and urinary bladder cancer in man: this is consistent with saccharin being neither a complete carcinogen nor a bladder tumour promoter in humans.' Yet the Committee itself made reference to a 1977 study which reported a 60 per cent increased risk of cancer of the bladder in males who consumed table-top sweeteners, but questioned the findings which were based on a small sample. It placed more weight on the results of a much bigger American study which showed no overall effect.

Over the years much has been written about the potential risks of cancer posed by some food colours made from coal tar. Ponceau 3R and ponceau MX were banned after liver cancers were discovered in mice and rats. Brilliant blue FCF and amaranth have both been suspected of possessing carcinogenic properties but the evidence has not been accepted in the UK and some other countries, and some experimental evidence was subsequently withdrawn.

Risks to pregnant women and unborn children

A few additives are mutagens – that is, they have been shown to cause damage to genetic material in cells; changes to reproductive cells may affect future generations. The evidence is limited, and most additives do not exhibit such effects. To date there is no direct evidence of ill-effects from additives on the unborn child, but where, in animal experiments, the foetus is affected, pregnant women may also be at risk. This is taken into account in assessments of safety. Saccharin has been accused of being toxic to pregnant women – the most common effects reported in the children of mothers known to have consumed saccharin during pregnancy were increased activity and irritability, and an extreme nervousness, although the effects do not seem to be lasting. Results from experiments in rats, rabbits and monkeys do not confirm the evidence of deformities found in one animal study. Even so, the possibility of effects suggests that pregnant women should be warned so that they can avoid saccharin if they wish.

The EEC recommended that warnings should be given on labels, but this has not been adopted.

Evidence that colouring agents may affect unborn children is very limited. One report from the USSR that amaranth was toxic to unborn rats at certain doses (considerably higher than the amounts consumed by humans) has caused concern, but this was not confirmed in US and UK studies.

Whether monosodium glutamate (MSG) can cause brain damage to a foetus is also controversial and experimental results are contradictory. At doses much higher than the maximum recommended human intake, it has been shown to induce nerve damage before birth in mice. Several studies show that new-born infants are at greater risk from MSG than adults, which is one reason why it is not permitted in baby food in the UK. Experiments in young rats and mice have shown severe brain damage, but young dogs and monkeys were not affected, and JECFA has recently given it clearance for use in unlimited amounts.

Mice fed the antioxidants BHA or BHT in their diet through mating and gestation produced young who appeared normal at birth, but developed abnormal growth and behavioural patterns when the antioxidants were also fed for three weeks during weaning. It was not clear whether the changes were the result of nerve damage, and if so, whether it occurred before or after birth.

Some scientists consider that there is a lot more work to be done in this field, but so far in the UK there is no requirement to advise pregnant women of any potential risk.

Problems with safety assessments and existing controls

Different expert opinion

Differences in the ways that additives are assessed for safety in different countries have caused a lot of public concern. The subject is highly complex: uncertainty surrounds much of the process of evaluation; scientists obtain different results in experiments; policy-makers recommend a variety of strategies on the basis of the evidence before them at different times. Consumers rely on scientists, food technologists and legislators to protect their interests, but when, for example, a substance is banned in one country in the wake of evidence of its carcinogenicity, but continues to be permitted in another, where it is considered to be 'safe', people don't know what to believe. The public is obliged to rely on experts' judgements about safety, but when experts can't agree, it's not surprising that consumers become sceptical.

There is a growing consensus among consumers that the use of additives should be permitted only when they are considered harmless and truly necessary, and otherwise that the numbers permitted should be reduced.

Problems with toxicological testing

Toxicology is not an exact science. Research on test animals in different countries at various times has produced conflicting results. In some instances differences have arisen from the lack of agreement about how to carry out experiments, or from insufficiently rigorous laboratory practice. In other cases, international opinion has questioned the quality of the source materials and the specifications of the additive tested.

Lack of independent testing

Most of the research carried out on particular additives is conducted by the companies who wish to market them, or by research organisations commissioned by industry to carry out the work. Neither the COT nor the SCF has authority to commission independent research to verify results, and can ask industry to carry out only the work which they believe is necessary. Since toxicological assessment is extremely expensive – it costs a minimum of £300,000 and takes three to four years to complete tests on a new additive – consumer organisations are not in any position to undertake such research. Such organisations are also excluded from the scientific committees at which results are questioned, so there is no built-in public scrutiny of the assessment procedures.

Recently, the Government has agreed to place any unpublished reports on which decisions have been based in the British Library, which at least will allow consumers and other scientists to examine the evidence once a recommendation has been made. However, this applies only to new additives and those that have been reviewed since 1986. Another drawback is that the information is made available only after the recommendations have been made.

Relevance of animal experiments for man

Since it is not ethical to carry out initial tests of new substances on humans, laboratory and animal experiments are used to assess risk. International protocols and EEC guidelines lay down precise stages and methods which should be followed in carrying out an assessment. However, inherent in the system are certain assumptions. In general, it is assumed that feeding experimental animals with a chemical over their lifetimes will give results which are relevant to consumption by people over their lifetimes; that the more of a chemical is given the greater the effect will be; and that the substance is safe for humans when no effect can be detected in animals.

Most public concern over additives focusses on the possibility that they may cause either cancer or adverse reactions, but it is very difficult to prove that an additive can cause cancer. The SCF stated in 1980 that it was not possible accurately to apply the results of animal tests directly to humans and gain an accurate result. Toxicologists themselves recognise that animal experiments have weaknesses, and research continues to try to improve the techniques. For example, the animal species being tested may not be sufficiently like humans to give useful evidence, or the chemical in question may interact with other chemicals which people are eating at the same time and cause an ill-effect which won't show up in animal studies. Applying any results to humans is always going to be difficult because the experimental animals have to be fed at very high doses, up to a maximum of 100 times that in the human diet. When toxic or other undesirable effects are found in test procedures, it is almost always at such exaggerated dose levels. It is then the role of the toxicologist to estimate the probability of a similar response at lower doses, and under normal conditions of consumption by humans.

Safety margins are applied to take account of variations

between species or between individual animals and people. The usual safety factor used to suggest the maximum acceptable human intake (ADI) is 100 times less than the amount shown to affect experimental animals, justified on the basis of a factor of 10 to allow for greater sensitivity in man, and a further 10 to allow for varied individual responses. It is a fairly arbitrary figure, but one that is thought to provide a sufficient safety margin. The safety factor of 100 is not applied in all circumstances, such as if the additive is an essential nutrient or a normal constituent of the body.

Where the quantities of an additive used are very small, as in the case of flavours and processing aids, the validity of using animal experiments to assess the lifetime risk for man is particularly questionable. Dr David Conning, Director of the British Nutrition Foundation has said: 'We have no way of knowing, using current methods, whether such materials can exert any deleterious effects over a protracted period of administration.' Dr Conning considered a major problem was the 'difficulty of predicting long-term consequences by using tests of relatively short duration. Man may consume an additive over 70 years, but even long-term animal experiments are likely to be no more than a few years at most.'

Animal tests are important, not least because substances cannot be tested on humans in the first instance. The EEC guidelines on the safety assessment of food additives recognise that despite their limitations, it is necessary to rely on investigations on laboratory animals. Where available, this can be backed up with information about the use of some additives for medicinal purposes or from tests on human volunteers.

The cocktail effect

So far it has not proved possible to test for the long-term health implications of consuming a wide variety of additives together. Yet in practice every day we eat additives in combination, and in increasing quantities. Some people consider that there may be an increased risk, known as 'the cocktail effect' where two or more additives may interact and cause problems which do not show up when testing one additive at a time.

The DHSS has said that testing additives individually is a

necessary simplification because it is a practical impossibility to test for the many combinations of additives to which people are exposed.

The European Parliament has called for safety evaluations to include assessments of the cocktail effect. Where substances such as tartrazine (E102), sodium benzoate (E211) and sulphur dioxide (E220), all of which are associated with adverse reactions, are used together as in the manufacture of soft drinks, it is not known whether the effects are exacerbated. Where additives are commonly used together, and particularly where they are sold as compound ingredients for use in individual products, they should be tested collectively too. Cost is always the deterrent.

A surfeit of additives?

Since there are no up-to-date studies on the subject, the question of whether people are damaging their health with a surfeit of additives cannot be answered with any confidence. People may regularly be exceeding recommended ADIs, for example of ammonia caramel colour (E150), sulphur dioxide (E220) and the benzoate preservatives (E210–19), but in the UK, the lack of relevant information, and failure to reassess additive intakes as tastes have changed, makes any comparison with ADIs impossible. Some people argue that the procedure is in any case unrealistic as we don't all eat the same foods on a regular basis.

Colours, and nitrites and nitrates, are the only additives whose consumption and use have been reviewed in recent years. The former showed that in a very few cases the ADI is likely to be exceeded, while the study of nitrites and nitrates noted that approximately 75 per cent of those we consume in food come from vegetable sources and derive from fertilisers, not additives. Further, the amounts used in cured meats have been consistently reduced. The Food Surveillance Unit of MAFF, which is responsible for studies of dietary intake, however, noted the need for more up-to-date information.

Occasionally eating more than the ADI for a single additive is unlikely to cause any harm, because the assessments incorporate a substantial safety factor. However, if governments permit manufacturers to use unlimited amounts of particular additives in foods which are consumed regularly or in large quantities, a substantial number of the population may regularly exceed the level of the ADI (particularly where the ADI is low). This is unacceptable and makes a nonsense of the procedures for establishing ADIs. It underlines the importance of regular review and reappraisal of how additives are used to ensure that the conditions of use, on which the safety assessments were made, remain valid.

In the UK, it appears that the quality of the diet has for too long been ignored in debates on additives. An unbalanced or unhealthy diet may have more serious consequences for the health of the population than the use of permitted additives themselves. Yet, within the DHSS, the Committee on the Medical Aspects of Food, which is responsible for advising the Government on nutrition and dietary questions, considers that additives are outside its brief. It does not, for example, examine whether the nutritional quality of food is lowered as a result of using certain food additives.

Insufficient and inadequate testing
Many additives were tested a long time ago under procedures less stringent than they are now. Furthermore, those additives which are not on permitted lists, such as flavours, enzymes and modified starches, have not been required to undergo testing by the COT at all. Some, such as clouding agents, modified starches and enzymes, have been looked at by the FAC in its attempt to review all outstanding additives, while others have been reviewed by JECFA. But the evaluations are by no means complete and the recommendations have not been implemented. So meanwhile, these additives need comply only with the general requirements of the Food Act 1984.

Weak regulations and lax control
Incomplete evaluation
Frequently, JECFA and the SCF are able to set only provisional ADIs because the results of long-term experiments are not available, or because the scientific data have not allowed a clear

conclusion to be drawn. They may also decide to review the additive again when further information is forthcoming. The COT may give such additives Group 'B' status (see earlier in the Chapter).

Further information requested by the COT within a limited period of time, such as two years, has often not been available, and this has resulted on many occasions in the additive continuing to be used for many years after its safety was first questioned. Some people feel strongly that when information is not forthcoming, or is insufficient to provide the necessary assurances, the additive should be deleted from the permitted list, the benefit of the doubt being given to the consumer.

Consumers' Association has said that if an additive already has category 'B' status and the additive research required to reassess it is not made available within a specified number of years, it should be banned. Additives which are not yet permitted would not be given category 'B' status; instead their approval would be delayed until the necessary evidence was made available. Others go further, saying that where doubts about safety exist the additive should be banned or severely restricted in use (rather than being given Group 'B' status) until it can be reassessed.

Risks to babies and young children

It is difficult to evaluate the extent to which legislators have taken account of the need for additional margins of safety where children are concerned. The Institute of Food Science and Technology (UK) notes that special consideration has been given to the particular susceptibility of infants and children, since they may be more or less susceptible to certain substances.

Twenty-six additives in the UK are prohibited in foods specially prepared for babies and young children because they are not needed or may not be safe. They include the antioxidants BHA (E320), BHT (E321) and the gallates (E310–12); the miscellaneous additives 2-aminoethanol and alpha-cellulose (E460b); the flavour enhancers MSG (621), guanosine 5'-(disodium phosphate) (627), inosine 5'-(disodium phosphate) (631) and sodium 5'-ribonucleotide (635); and polydextrose. The nitrite and nitrate preservatives are banned in food for babies and young children, as are the artificial sweeteners. In the past the FAC has also recommended that starches modified by epichlorohydrin and/or propylene oxide should not be used in foods for infants and young children, while certain other modified starches should have restricted use. These proposals have not been made into regulations.

The legislation has been extended in 1988 to prohibit the use of colours in baby food, giving statutory effect to a voluntary ban which has been operated by the manufacturers for some years. Only three colours will in future be permitted in baby food – riboflavin (E101), riboflavin 5'-phosphate (101a) and the carotenes (E160a), all of which are vitamins.

The problem is that while these regulations protect very young children, most children from about one year old consume a diet which increasingly resembles that of adults, and they may not be sufficiently well developed to cope with the quantities of additives contained in our food. MAFF considers that with the exception of those additives which are prohibited in baby and infant food, the rest are safe for general use. The DHSS does not appear to be so sure. It says that by the age of three a child's digestive system, liver and kidneys should be able to cope with the full range of additives. But what of the child between one and three who is eating foods other than those specifically intended for young children?

Many of the foods regularly eaten by young children contain additives banned from baby foods. Some soft drinks and ready-made desserts, for example, contain artificial sweeteners, banned from baby foods. Many of the snacks marketed specifically for children contain MSG, and some still have the antioxidants BHA and BHT which are prohibited in infant food (although these have to a large extent been removed during the past two years).

Are natural additives any safer than artificial ones?

As a result of people's concern about additives, there has been a widespread and largely unchecked move from those additives considered unacceptable by consumers towards so-called 'natural' alternatives. But, as the FAC and the COT have stressed, the fact that they are of natural origin does not make them inherently safe.

In addition, the IFST states that there is a valid reason for discriminating between additives which are natural food components and those which are not. 'It is possible that the human metabolism may have adapted to those substances frequently encountered and hence have a defensive mechanism. For other substances . . . man may not have a satisfactory defensive system.'

Although in the UK all substances on permitted lists, whether of natural or synthetic origin, have been assessed by the COT, the toxicity of many natural additives has not yet been established with the same degree of precision as has been required of the synthetic additives. Many of the natural additives which are also naturally present in food have been tested to a lesser extent or, being generally recognised as safe, were tested and approved many years ago under procedures which were less rigorous than those in use today. Because they are from natural sources, the chemical composition of these additives may vary, depending on the climate, the soil conditions, the season, and other factors affecting their environment. The specifications for synthetic additives are very precise and are on the whole laid down in regulations.

A further concern is that to achieve the desired effect, far higher quantities of natural additives may have to be used than the synthetic alternatives. The long-term effects of recent increases in consumption have not so far been considered by the authorities, although for many additives of natural origin JECFA has indicated that it does not consider it appropriate or necessary to set an upper limit to the ADI since the substance is widely consumed in unprocessed foods. This approach may not be the most appropriate for substances added to foods which have little nutritional benefit.

Much of the research into new additives is concentrating on developing additives from natural source materials so that a label stating 'no artificial additives' or 'natural additives only' can give a marketing advantage. For example, carotene (E160a), an orangey-red colour is found in carrots, apricots, rosehips, oranges and tomatoes. It may be extracted from carrots using a solvent, and may contain processing residues, oils, fats and waxes from the source.

Although the source material may be from a plant, tree, or naturally occurring substance, the source itself may not be edible, and may not be from the plant with which the consumer would associate the product. Thus, almond flavour may be extracted from peach and apricot kernels, not almonds.

Many of the additives currently in use are actually nature-identical. That is, they are produced entirely under laboratory conditions to replicate, as closely as possible, the chemical structure of the natural additive. (Artificial additives are substances for which no equivalent substance exists or has been detected in nature.)

There is no straightforward answer as to whether nature-identical additives are more or less safe than the synthetic or natural varieties. Some people say that natural additives could be potentially more dangerous than synthetic. For example, flavours and colours could vary in composition, or they may deteriorate over time. Because of such variations, they may also require the addition of stabilisers or antioxidants to preserve them in a satisfactory state. Substances extracted from plants may react differently when digested as an additive and when digested as part of a plant. Research into this question is only just beginning.

Conclusion

Many of the factors outlined above are considered every time an assessment is made of the safety of an additive for use in food. The toxicological assessment then has to be weighed against any potential risk to the population from not using the additive, and the extent to which it is needed. The final judgement on such risk/benefit assessments in the UK is left in the hands of the Ministers of Health and of Agriculture, Fisheries and Food acting as co-signatories on legislation, and on the advice of the relevant advisory committees.

The decisions are only as sound as the advice and scientific information available, which in turn depends on the funding available for testing. The *BIBRA* Bulletin* noted in June 1986 that the more animal species an additive is tested in, the greater confidence there would be in estimates of how it might affect people. The greater the knowledge about the mechanism of an effect found in animals, the more profound the evaluation. But these require even more expenditure on testing. The authors of the article considered that 'the present arrangements of testing and evaluation . . . are probably adequately protecting most of the population from most of the potential toxic action of additives' but the public have not been asked whether they think the resources are wisely or most effectively spent. The public meet the bill in the cost of food, and would pay the price of inadequate safety standards in the medical costs which could arise from food poisoning, adverse reactions and other medical conditions.

Generally, the scientific community is cautious in its approach. Neither manufacturers nor retailers can afford to risk a death, directly attributable to an additive, as happened when sulphur dioxide (E220) was used on fresh food in catering establishments in the United States, a use which is not permitted in the UK.

The UK Government certainly gives the appearance of being less stringent than some other countries in the number of additives which it continues to permit, and in allowing additives for which toxicological information is incomplete to remain on permitted lists. Some feel strongly that the authorities have failed to respond adequately, in particular to the needs of those with adverse reactions, while others are equally convinced that the issue has been exaggerated out of all proportion. How safe additives are perceived to be remains a matter of judgement.

* British Industrial Biological Research Association.

3
What's on the label?

People are encouraged by the Ministry of Agriculture, Fisheries and Food and the food industry to look at package labels in order to identify which additives are used in foods: the vast majority of additives do appear on labels but there are significant exceptions which are explored below. The arguments concern the costs and benefits of full labelling: should there be a limit on the consumer's right to know what is in the food he or she eats? The minority who suffer adverse reactions clearly need to know, but should the costs of this be borne by the population as a whole? Whether you choose to avoid certain additives or need to do so on medical grounds the real question is whether it's possible to identify what's present.

Additives which appear on labels

Ingredients lists – introducing additives
Under the Food Labelling Regulations 1984, prepacked and processed foods for retail sale (with certain exceptions) must carry a list of ingredients, including any additives used. Additives are substances added to, or used in or on, food which affect its keeping qualities, texture, consistency, appearance, taste, odour, alkalinity or acidity, or serve any other technological function in relation to food. In other words, an additive is something in food which you would not consume as a food on its own.

Ingredients must be listed in descending order of weight in the finished product so that people can identify the main elements. Hence, in a carton of orange drink, the main ingredients are water, orange juice and sugar, so appear first. Additives are often used in comparatively small quantities, so come low in the order of ingredients.

Category names

Additives must be labelled, in most cases, according to the function they perform. Seventeen categories of additives are covered in this way:

Acids	Flavourings
Acidity regulators	Flour improvers
Anti-caking agents	Gelling agents
Anti-foaming agents	Glazing agents
Antioxidants	Preservatives
Artificial sweeteners	Raising agents
Colours	Stabilisers
Emulsifiers	Thickeners
Flavour enhancers	

Many additives can achieve more that one effect in foods, and are used for different purposes in different products. Where an additive can serve more than one function, the category declared must be the principal function which it performs in that particular food.

Since a permitted additive may be used for any purpose, the function declared on the label may not be the one under which it was originally regulated. For example, sulphur dioxide (E220) appears on a permitted list as a preservative but it can also be used as a flour improver or to stabilise wine.

Names and 'E' numbers

With the exception of flavourings, additives must also be quoted by their specific name, or number, or both. The EEC has established numbers for about 280 permitted additives as a short-hand for the chemical names. Some additives which have not been fully considered within the Community have serial numbers without the 'E' prefix. Hence, the label may specify 'colour, carmoisine'; or 'colour E122'; or 'colour, carmoisine (E122)'. In the case of monosodium glutamate, the label may read 'flavour enhancer 621'; or 'flavour enhancer: monosodium glutamate'; or 'flavour enhancer 621, monosodium glutamate'.

In general, colourings have numbers between E100 and E199; preservatives E200–E299; antioxidants and antioxidant synergists (additives which increase the effect of others) E300–E399; and emulsifiers, stabilisers, thickeners and gelling agents E400–E499. All the 'E' numbers tell you is that the additive has been approved and is permitted for use in the EEC. The absence of an 'E' may mean either:

- that the particular additive has not been fully evaluated for use in the EEC, although it is approved in the UK, *or*
- that the particular class of additives has not yet been regulated by the EEC.

Many food additives do not yet have 'E' numbers (although more will do so in due course). In addition, there are as many as 3,500 flavourings which do not have to be declared by name or number, but need be described only by the category name. Any additive which does not perform one of the functions listed above, which is used in food but for which no precise regulations apply (such as an enzyme or clouding agent – see Chapter 9), must be declared by its full name.

Full names or 'E' numbers?

When 'E' numbers first appeared on food labels in 1986, little public information was available to explain what they meant or why all additives were now being listed on food labels. They had always been in the food, it was just that now food manufacturers were obliged to tell consumers what had gone into it. Retailers found customers associating 'E' numbers not with 'Europe' or 'evaluated' but with 'evil', and some people tried to avoid all products containing 'E' numbers, while unwittingly eating others containing additives not yet reviewed by the EEC.

Because of public concern that products containing additives with 'E' numbers are to be avoided, many manufacturers and retailers are now giving the full chemical names, except when an additive's name is itself notorious, such as tartrazine – in this case, people are known to be looking out for it, so E102 is thought preferable by some manufacturers. This has led to the undesirable and confusing practice of mixing the descriptions of additives – some with names, others with numbers – on the same label.

It would be far better if manufacturers quoted 'E' numbers where these had been allocated, so that people could become used to the system and be able to compare two labels like for like.

One commentator who works in a food manufacturing company has written: 'Many manufacturers and retailers would probably be far better off in the longer term by using only the "E" numbers, so that this means of declaration became the standard practice throughout the food industry and the current unscientific and potentially misleading competitive activity would be avoided.'

When is an 'ingredient' an 'additive'?

It is difficult to tell from labels which ingredients are 'foods' as defined in the regulations and which are additives. The definition of additive quoted at the beginning of the Chapter excludes vitamins and minerals added for nutritional purposes: herbs, spices and starches which are considered to be foods in their own right.

One of the few ways of telling which items on an ingredients list are additives lies in the category name, such as 'preservative' or 'emulsifier', which precedes the number or name. But this is not foolproof: for example, citric acid (E330) can appear on the label without its category 'acid' since the word 'acid' is part of its name. Citric acid may be used for several purposes, such as to help achieve a set in jam or to increase the effect of anti-oxidants, and yet it appears under its name alone, or perhaps with one category name. Furthermore, although it would be potentially misleading and technically incorrect, citric acid might be declared as lemon juice if that was the main source. As another example, vinegar has preservative functions and is increasingly used, for example, to replace other preservatives in bread. Vinegar is classed as a food, and is not a permitted additive. Hence, it can be included in the ingredients list without any reference to its function, allowing the claim to be made that the product contains 'no artificial preservatives'.

Understanding the label

Here are examples of two ingredients lists. They show what the manufacturer has used to produce the food, in order of the amount used: the first ingredient listed is used in the greatest amount, the last one in the smallest amount.

Black Forest gateau

Ingredients

Dairy cream, sugar, chocolate flavour strands (contain emulsifier E322), glazing agents 904, E414, flour, skimmed milk, egg, glacé cherries (contain preservatives E202, E220, colour E127), morello cherries, vegetable fat, cocoa, dextrose, cornflour, modified starch, soya flour, emulsifiers (E322, E471, E457, 476), salt, stabilisers (E401, E465), colours (155, E102, E110, E122, E123, E124, E132, E142, E151), kirsch, flavourings, gelling agent (E410), acidity regulator (E331), preservative (E211).

The ingredients list must include all additives which perform a function in the final product.

Modified starches are indicated only by the generic name 'modified starch'.

Some serial numbers do not have an 'E' prefix because the additives have not been fully evaluated by the European Community.

E410 locust bean gum is a permitted stabiliser but is used here as a gelling agent.

The category name must be accompanied by either the serial number identifying the additive or its chemical name (or both) for most categories of additives. For this label, the manufacturer has chosen the serial numbers.

Dextrose (glucose) and salt are not classed as additives.

Only the category name need be used for flavourings.

Whole orange drink

Ingredients
(after dilution)

Water, sugar, glucose syrup, comminuted oranges, citric acid, preservatives sodium benzoate and sodium metabisulphite, artificial sweetener (saccharin), vitamin C, flavourings, colour (beta-carotene – provides vitamin A).

The food manufacturer has chosen to use the chemical names of additives instead of their serial numbers.

Vitamin C is the same chemical as the antioxidant E300 – ascorbic acid. Here, however, it is being used as a vitamin.

It is not necessary to use the category name for additives which function as 'acids' in foods, and whose chemical name includes the word 'acid'.

Saccharin does not have a serial number so it must be indicated by the category – 'artificial sweetener' – *and* its chemical name.

Although beta-carotene is a permitted colour, and is being used as a colour in this drink, it is also a source of vitamin A.

Source – MAFF *Food additives: The balanced approach* 1987.

Labelling anomalies and exclusions

The vast majority of additives appear on labels but there are certain significant exceptions.

Certain pre-packed products

Several categories of food and drink are excluded from the food labelling regulations for a variety of reasons. Some of these are single ingredient products, such as honey and milk, which are exempt because their labelling is directly controlled by EEC regulations or because their content has been precisely defined in the UK. Others are coffee, cocoa and chocolate products, and certain milk products. Eggs and wine are considered by the EEC to be agricultural commodities and so are also exempt. The labelling requirements for all these items vary and may be less comprehensive than for food in general.

The FAC in its report on food labelling in 1979 said that in the past it was generally accepted that if the composition of a food were controlled by law, the consumer would be adequately protected and would know what to expect from the product – so the ingredients did not need to appear on any label. However, this was now no longer defensible because consumers might not know why some foods were exempt from labelling, nor be in a position to visit a public library to find out the products covered by compositional standards, and what a staple product should legally contain. As a matter of principle, the FAC recommended that there should be no exemptions from the requirement to declare ingredients. Yet exemptions still exist.

The only additives which have to be declared on butter, cheese, fermented milk and cream are those which are not essential to the manufacturing process. For instance, cheese may merely state: 'Added colour, annatto' and not the full list of ingredients.

Equally, where additives have been used in the feed of chickens to colour egg yolks or that of salmon or trout to make the flesh pink, this does not have to be declared, but, in Consumers' Association's view, should be.

Unwrapped foods, small packets, and those sold for immediate consumption

Pre-packed bread must be labelled, but bread which is pre-packed on the store premises or is sold unwrapped need only be labelled with the name of the product. The same applies to cakes, pastries and sweets which are unwrapped or packed in wholly transparent packaging for sale in the shops where they were baked. Yet nowadays in-store packaging may well include labelling with a description of the product as well as its name and certain required categories of additives, so why should it not also contain a comprehensive list of ingredients?

Sweets, chocolate confectionery and individual biscuits or cakes which are sold unwrapped or in small packets with an area of less than 10 square centimetres are exempt from some of the requirements, as are products sold from vending machines.

Individually wrapped ice-creams or lollies, sandwiches, rolls, hot pies and pasties, cakes, biscuits or pieces of quiche intended for immediate consumption and sold from a shop, mobile vehicle or catering establishment must indicate the name of the product, but need not contain a precise list of ingredients.

At present, where shops sell wet fish, delicatessen foods such as fresh cooked meats, unpacked salads, and other unwrapped products which contain additives, the food itself need not be fully labelled, but, if not, retailers are required to indicate on a ticket if certain categories of additive are present. Alternatively, a notice should be displayed 'in close proximity to' the food – a sign on the wall behind would not be considered close enough.

While some retailers oppose any extension of the labelling regulations, and are conscious of the difficulties of making the information about delicatessen products, for instance, legible and clear in cabinets with many products, there are other ways of providing the information. Retailers could use wall space for displaying factual information as well as advertising. Printed sheets of information about the content of fresh and cooked foods in delicatessens might also be produced for customers who want them. If the law required such information to be fully displayed or made available in all retail outlets, the suppliers or trade associations would have to make appropriate information available to retailers.

The FAC has maintained that labelling laws for pre-packed food should be stricter than those for food which isn't pre-packed. It wanted for practical reasons to avoid food being 'festooned with tickets which would detract from the main information'. It has also been suggested that small businesses would face an intolerable burden if all food was subject to the same laws on ingredient labelling. But from the consumer's point of view, it is just as important to know what is in foods which are sold unwrapped as it is to know about wrapped foods.

Alcoholic drinks

Alcoholic drinks were excluded from the ingredient listing provisions in the labelling regulations in 1970 (along with confectionery and biscuits) on the grounds that there were major difficulties for manufacturers and 'little advantage to consumers' in declaring the ingredients. The brewing and wine-making industry has been united in its refusal to give consumer groups information about ingredients (although one told us that it would release such information to a person with particular health problems). As one manufacturer argued to us: 'There have recently been suggestions from commentators who, perhaps, do not fully understand the scientific complexity of the brewing and fermenting processes, that beer should be subject to ingredient labelling. You will doubtless be aware that the changes that occur during fermentation are such that the final composition of the product reaching the consumer is significantly different to that of the raw materials at the start of the process.' For this reason the company does not support the labelling proposals, 'but prefers to rely on its integrity as the most successful brewery company in the UK.' Such companies should have nothing to fear from telling consumers what their brews contain. The EEC plans to introduce legislation in this area, and in the United States, from January 1988, an indication of the presence of sulphur dioxide in wine has become mandatory on health grounds.

In the UK today, beer and lager may legally contain a range of additives including gypsum or Epsom salts to make the water more like that from Burton (the origin of some of Britain's most famous beers); colour such as tartrazine (in lager), caramel or burnt sugar to darken the brew; carrageenan (which comes from seaweed) and isinglass to clarify it and give a traditional texture; and ascorbic acid (vitamin C) to lengthen its shelf-life. Some of these are processing aids which may leave very small amounts of residue in the drink. Yet none of these need be declared.

Germany has recently lost a campaign to maintain the purity of beer on sale by allowing only water, yeast, hops and barley malt as ingredients and to prevent the importation of brews containing additives. It is likely that the German population may be able to choose from a wider variety of beers in the future, but unless regulations for labelling are introduced they will no longer know what's in them, and the quality could be reduced.

Within the EEC, a wide range of additives may also be used in wine-making, and these likewise remain undeclared. They include sulphur which stops oxidation and the growth of micro-organisms; cultured yeasts to control fermentation; yeast feeders; citric acid to stabilise the wine; metatartaric acid and potassium bitartrate to take out the acid; tannin to preserve red wine; copper sulphate to reduce sulphide; and carbon dioxide to put bubbles into cheap sparkling wine.

Processing aids and ingredients carried over

Processing aids used to assist the manufacturer, such as tin-greasing emulsions to stop products sticking to machines, free-flow agents to speed the movement of a product through machinery, solvents used to carry flavours or colours and disperse them in a food, or to extract elements such as caffeine, do not have to be declared; nor do enzymes for tenderising meat, processing sugar, clarifying fruit juice or conditioning beer where they are used as processing aids. When added at a later stage in the processing, they should be declared. Processing aids only have to be declared when the additives perform a function in the final product. However, where some processing aids – notably the solvents that carry colours and flavours – are present at significant levels, it could be argued that they should be identified on the label.

When the FAC made its recommendations that processing aids need not be labelled, people's interest in and knowledge of food labelling was considerably less than it is today. Some legislation, such as the EEC Directive on Solvents, recognises that it is almost impossible to exclude all residues in the final product, and a small number of people may be sensitive to minimal amounts of certain substances. If labelling is to be comprehensive, consideration should be given to including processing aids.

Some additives may be present in small amounts because they were contained in ingredients used to make another product. They do not have to be declared if they are not added directly to the final product, and serve no function in it. For example, sulphite solution is used to preserve fruit so that it can be used in jam-making throughout the year. Most of the preservative evaporates in the steam when the jam is being made, but a limited amount remains. This is carried over into the food but does not have to be declared on the jar's label. Similarly, the fruit used in muesli may have been treated with mineral oils to stop it sticking together, or preserved with sulphur dioxide, but this is not necessarily stated on the muesli packaging.

Retailers and manufacturers themselves may not be aware of the existence of such residues, and although some companies make it their business to know, and ask for details of all ingredients to be made known in the product specifications, consumers are no wiser if the information isn't conveyed on the label. Although it is much more difficult for small wholesalers and retailers than large supermarkets to obtain information on additives used in ingredients, they would be able to demand the information if food labels were required to include it by law.

Additive claims

Artificial or natural – does it matter?

Essential information which companies must put on the label is defined by regulations. Beyond that, packagers may include more or less what they wish, provided it is true and does not mislead. The public concern about additives has led to a rush of claims from manufacturers showing what they consider to be the 'positive' aspects of their products with flashes such as 'No artificial colours' or 'No artificial additives'. Some people may interpret 'no artificial' as 'additive-free' whereas it is likely to mean exactly what it says and nothing more: there will probably be natural additives in the product – otherwise the flash would say 'Additive free'.

In general, manufacturers and retailers have exploited the public prejudice against 'E' numbers, which are in some cases wrongly thought to be artificial chemicals, and therefore 'bad'; on the other hand they have emphasised the 'natural' and hence 'good' additives or ingredients in their products. Different companies have different policies on how they label, and some are nearer than others to the margin where they could mislead consumers. A claim such as 'no added preservative' may be used by some retailers where no preservative was added during manufacture of the final product, although it was already present in one of the ingredients, but it would have to be declared if it were performing a preservative function. The claim for 'no preservative' may also be made by some who have replaced a 'preservative' with an 'antioxidant', or who are using an ingredient (such as vinegar) to achieve a preservative effect.

Manufacturers and retailers are also trying to enhance the 'natural' image of products by using phrases such as 'grape extract' rather than anthocyanins (E163) on ingredient lists, and describing colouring or flavouring with the adjective 'natural'. MAFF has suggested that both these practices may be illegal. The description 'natural colours curcumin, annatto, anthocyanins' on a peach melba sundae is purely to gain a marketing advantage, and may mislead customers about the origin or status of the additives. A confectionery manufacturer commented to us: 'We ourselves are somewhat concerned about the misleading claims often made in the labelling of food products, and do not make claims as to any natural or otherwise attributes of our products. In this respect, we would like to see labelling regulations changed in order to avoid the confusion.'

Many of the flavours and colours currently labelled 'natural' are actually 'nature-identical': they may have been created to the same or similar chemical structure to a colour or flavour which comes from a product derived directly from nature, but may be synthesised under laboratory conditions and not have any ingredients which you would normally consume in food.

For natural additives need not come from the food source with which the customer would associate the additive. Although beta-carotene can be found in carrots or tomatoes, a natural beta-carotene additive would rarely come from either source – yet it might well be used to colour a carrot or tomato product. Almond flavour may come from peach or apricot kernels. Furthermore, the additive may be used in a context which is not 'natural' such as putting flavour and colour in a milk drink.

Some people mistakenly believe that any additive which has an 'E' number is 'artificial', while anything labelled by its full name is 'natural'. Research carried out on behalf of the Presto company (*Eating what comes naturally?*) required housewives to consider the lists of ingredients in two unnamed foods – in fact, identical fish pies. On one packet additives were identified by 'E' numbers and on the other by their specific names. The housewives were asked which they considered to be more natural. Forty-five per cent opted for the product with names, only 8 per cent for the one in which the additives were identified by their 'E' numbers.

The presence of 'E' numbers, and the fact that an additive is regulated, does not tell you anything about the origin of the substance. Permitted additives may be either synthetic, nature-identical, or natural in origin. You cannot tell from the description what the source was.

It is a mistake to believe that additives labelled 'natural' are inherently better, preferable or safer than artificial additives; all additives are chemical substances and all should be thoroughly tested for safety. The FAC has suggested that voluntary guidelines be introduced to limit the use of the word 'natural'. If put into practice, this would mean that the word 'natural' applied only to additives obtained from recognised food sources and extracted by physical rather than chemical means, and to flavourings only when they originated from the named food source. Such guidelines would at least reduce some of the current confusion.

Labelling policies

In Chapter 10 we describe the policies that many of the major supermarkets put into practice. All admit that their response to people's demand for more information on additives has been largely a marketing exercise, and the result has been increased competition for the most attractive rather than the most precise claims.

Most companies say that they do not use claims such as 'free from' if residues on particular ingredients could have been carried over, but not all have sufficient control over their suppliers to be absolutely certain. Most companies are not explicit about whether they label additives which are carried over from ingredients, and they label processing aids only where the aid also has a function in the final product, such as free-flow agents in salt. But Tesco and Waitrose claim that they always declare carry-over.

Sainsbury's have a clearly defined policy on what may be labelled and how. They allow claims for 'No added . . .' to be used only where this attribute makes it different from most other equivalent foods on the market, or when the product has been modified in some way. They will not allow products which, for example, have never been coloured to use a 'No added colour' flash.

Safeway declare carry-over where the residue is more than one part per million, and will use claims that a product is 'free from' a particular additive only when it has not been used anywhere in the food chain. While Bejam also declare this to be their policy, they are aware that they do not have total control over the food chain, unlike Iceland who place very stringent requirements on their suppliers and trace all additives back to source. Bejam take the view that since the law permits processing aids to be used, the company cannot prohibit it. Other retailers take a stronger line. Nurdin and Peacock, who supply independent retailers, encourage ingredient declarations beyond the minimum required by law and are concerned that the phrase 'No added . . .' may mislead consumers since the additives may be in ingredients. So the overall situation remains unclear.

Because of the speed with which companies have tried to remove artificial colours (in particular), and the rate at which product specifications have been revised, we found that in some cases packaging did not reflect the new specifications. Several companies admitted that packaging is very expensive, and substantial stocks were held. Thus 'it had proved necessary to go on using old packaging although new ingredients were being used'. Trading standards officers, short of resources to enforce food law, had turned a blind eye to this temporary situation on the understanding that the 'quality' of products had been improved by the removal of some additives, and in the knowledge that people would not be harmed by the changes, and that increased packaging costs would be passed on to consumers.

Recognising the value which customers place on informative labelling, some manufacturers are going further than the legislation requires. One sausage manufacturer is now specifying which ingredients constitute less than 1 per cent of the contents, most of which are additives, and goes on to explain that of these 'triphosphates' are 'to keep product texture', 'antioxidants – to prevent discoloration'. The extra-lean variety packaging claims: 'These sausages contain the minimum necessary additives to ensure product perfection' – all this information is clearly intended to reassure purchasers.

Why label?

Aren't ingredients lists enough?

In response to concerns about allergic reactions, several companies have computerised information about the ingredients and additives contained in their products, which customers can write for. Some companies can give a comprehensive list of all own-label products which are free from artificial additives, but these are in the minority. When we asked for such information we found that some companies supplied information just on products without added colour, or without artificial colour or flavouring. Some had lists of those which were free from preservatives, and a few those which were free from monosodium glutamate. All stressed that the product ranges frequently change and the lists soon become out of date. Most lists were too long to carry with you while doing the week's shopping.

The right to informative labelling

In 1979 the FAC stated that people have a right to know what is in the food they eat, and moreover to be able to discriminate between products at a glance, without having to carry out their own taste and quality tests. Labels should not mislead people by leaving out relevant information.

Consumers' Association wants to bring an end to some of the current exemptions. There should be full ingredients listing for wine, beer and chocolates, and consideration given to the possibility of including small packets of food, snacks and sandwiches. CA recognises the problems that retailers face but consumers' needs are the same whether foods are packed or loose. Information should be available on printed sheets for products sold unpacked but while that is not available shoppers wanting to avoid additives will have to buy pre-packed varieties.

Safety for those at risk

Labelling is not only about exercising choice, and ensuring you are not deceived or exploited – it is about identifying substances which for a small number of people are known to be harmful and, for some, potentially lethal. This is, of course, as valid for products containing egg, gluten or soya as those containing sulphur dioxide or tartrazine.

The lack of a reference to the additive on the label may mislead people into thinking that a product is free from it when traces remain. Although for most people the omission will not affect their health, they may still wish to make comparisons with other products. Others who are highly sensitive, for instance to sulphur dioxide, need to know if the fruit in their jam or squash has been so treated.

Despite thorough-going recommendations from the FAC, the Food Labelling Regulations 1984 fell short of what was recommended, and people are inadequately protected and informed as a result. Labelling of additives is incomplete, and does not at present meet the objective of ensuring that people know what is in the food they eat.

4
A riot of colours

Colouring agents are widely used in the manufacture of sweets, cakes and biscuits, soft drinks, jellies, dairy products (milk, yoghurts and ice-creams, for example), processed desserts, jams, pickles, preserves, sauces, relishes and alcoholic drinks. The main reason for adding colour to such products is to increase their aesthetic appeal.

In recent years colours have attracted more attention than any other additives. They have given rise to such controversy partly because they are the most obviously cosmetic and partly because people have been made aware of a connection between some artificial dyes and adverse reactions to food.

The use of colouring agents is regulated by the European Community as well as the UK. All permitted colours have a number, though not all have been allocated an 'E' prefix. Colours are numbered within the range E100 – E199 (see the list at the back of the book). The regulations do not, however, distinguish between colours of natural and synthetic origin.

Colours may be of natural origin, nature-identical or synthetic. The main natural colours come from pigments which occur in plant and animal tissues. They include:

- **carotenoids** Yellow to orange-red colours which are found in abundance in, for instance, apricots, carrots, oranges, corn, peaches and tomatoes and in the skins of bananas
- **chlorophylls** The green pigment contained in the leaves and stems of plants
- **anthocyanins** Red, blue and violet pigments found in beetroots, plums, raspberries, red cabbage and black grape skins

- **flavones** Yellow pigments that can be found in the leaves and petals of almost every plant
- **sugar** When heat-treated, a chemical reaction occurs, leading to the brown colour found in caramel.

Twenty synthetic colours are permitted of which the **azo dyes** form the main group. They include tartrazine (E102), sunset yellow (E110), carmoisine (E122), amaranth (E123), ponceau 4R (E124) and black PN (E151).

In addition to the numbered colours, food manufacturers may also use any of the following ingredients as colouring agents although they also have other properties, for example as flavours: paprika, saffron, crocin, sandalwood, santalin and turmeric. It is not always clear how these substances should be labelled.

Company policies

Widespread removal of colour

Since 1985 or so, in response to changes in demand, there has been a substantial change in companies' policies towards the use of additives in general and towards colours in particular. One company which we approached recalled: 'Colours in the past were added indiscriminately. For example, up to six could be used in a single biscuit.' Some retail and manufacturing companies have now removed colours completely from some products. Examples include vanilla ice-cream, certain brands of ready-mixed drinks, squashes, peas and yoghurts. Many mixer drinks do not now contain added colour, and rely instead on colour from natural juices. One company produces cider without added colour. It is no longer the norm to add caramel to brown bread and bread flour, although it can still be found in some speciality loaves and malt breads. Many more colour-free products are available now than at the start of the 1980s.

Change from synthetic to natural

Public pressure has brought about a shift away from synthetic substances in favour of natural or nature-identical varieties. For major retailers who have actively tried to limit the use of unnecessary additives, a review of colouring agents has been the main priority. They have all made a significant effort to replace the synthetic colours in their products, although they have followed different policies. Some companies produced a list of those colours which they wished suppliers to remove from all their own-label varieties. Others wished to minimise the use of artificial colours and asked for them to be removed 'wherever possible'. A third group stated that no synthetic colours were to be used in new products.

Options available

Most companies have had to choose between removing colouring altogether or replacing it with a natural alternative. Hence, some no longer add any colour to batters, fish coatings and smoked fish, while others are using turmeric or paprika instead of the original synthetic colours. Where kippers continue to be coloured, annatto (E160) has replaced tartrazine (E102), while in smoked cod and haddock, tartrazine and sunset yellow (E110) are currently being replaced by crocin, which is obtained from saffron. Uncoloured vanilla ice-cream is now available, but some companies are replacing tartrazine with curcumin, turmeric or carotene (E160a) to retain a creamy appearance. Some strawberry and ripple ices also now use natural colours. Several retailers sell canned peas without added colour. Others maintain that this would be unacceptable to their customers. Some companies have never had colour, for example, in canned fruits, while others claim the need for them. Claims for colour-free products may include some of those which traditionally were not coloured. The removal of some colours has been assisted by improved processing and packaging techniques.

The change in attitude to the need for colour has been substantial, but it is impossible to quantify the extent of the change; the majority of products are anyway still coloured. Colour-free varieties are commonly sold alongside alternatives containing natural or synthetic colour. This is particularly true of sweets, squashes, cake mixes and instant desserts. It is usually possible to obtain products without colour, although not necessarily the brand of your choice, and you may have to purchase a frozen or chilled variety rather than a canned or dried one.

Consumers' needs

Whether you want to buy products which are coloured or not is a matter of personal preference. Manufacturers cater to the range of preferences in a variety of ways.

Psychological need

If food is unattractive, consumers will not want to eat it. As the FAC commented in 1979: 'We recognise that colour plays a significant part in our enjoyment of food as, indeed, it does in our enjoyment of other facets of our lives.' The SCF went slightly further in claiming that consumers had a 'psychological need' for their food to be coloured. But that does not necessarily mean that food needs to be artificially coloured – while consumers clearly want attractive food, colour can be present in the natural ingredients.

Demand for natural rather than artificial colours to be used in food has had a profound effect on marketing practice. In 1979, the FAC cited the example of a firm of retailers who found that sales fell by 50 per cent when they stopped putting colour into canned peas, strawberries and jams. Although the colour was reinstated, it took two years before previous sales were regained. A salutary lesson was learnt – namely, that consumers need to have the reasons for such changes explained, and want to be consulted in the process.

By the mid-1980s, however, the situation was quite different. An increasing number of consumers sought products either without added colour or with the artificial colours removed. So considerable was the opposition to the synthetic dye tartrazine (E102) that some retailers considered it a liability to sell products containing it. Several asked manufacturers to exclude it from own-brand products. Consumers have come to accept paler products, and find foods such as smoked fish or yoghurt acceptable with no added colour – indeed some consumers prefer them.

There has always been a close association in people's minds between colour and flavour. Colour helps us distinguish lager from stout, Cheddar from red Leicester, and brown bread from white. The associations develop early in childhood. Tests have shown that people are unable to identify the flavour of foods which are wrongly coloured, such as a red lemon-flavoured jelly or mousse, and coloured solutions are perceived as having a stronger flavour than colourless liquids.

Choice and variety

Colours have been extensively used, often in association with flavours, to increase the variety and range of products. For example, without added colour and flavour, the range of instant desserts would have been much more limited; and while, in theory, different flavours could have been sufficient to provide choice, in practice people associate flavour with colour. One company which removed colour from its orange and lemon drinks had complaints that they looked the same when diluted. Since only a small number of natural colours are suitable for use in products which have clear packaging and can be affected by light, it is difficult to ensure that the naturally coloured foods can be differentiated by colour.

To provide additional choice, manufacturers use colour in some products which previously did not contain it. Coloured sugar crystals, for example, are produced as a speciality for sweetening drinks or to decorate cakes and desserts. They are not essential, but meet the demand for speciality uses.

Consumers want a choice of products of varying quality and price to meet their particular needs, but colour may be used to disguise differences in quality of otherwise similar products. Hence, many manufacturers continue to use the colour red 2G in sausages and sausage-based products to suggest the presence of more meat than there actually is. Some manufacturers argue that consumers want pork sausages, for example, to look different in colour from beef, but that without added colour they would be virtually indistinguishable. Others have found uncoloured sausages and pies impossible to sell because the normal brown colour is associated with a loss of freshness and quality. As consumer groups have pointed out, the use of colour enables the fat content of sausages to be increased, and consumers could be misled about the meat content. Colour in lemon or orange flavour desserts may also make it appear that fruit has been used when it is absent, or when it has been included in only small quantities.

There are a few products which would not exist at all, or in which the range would be significantly reduced, without added colour: they are mainly foods which are not essential for nutrition – so you could choose not to eat them at all. Confectionery such as fruit flavour gums and boiled sweets would be much more expensive, and possibly uneconomic to make, if real fruits rather than additives were used to provide colour. The range of flavoured drinks would be more limited and possibly more expensive.

Manufacturers' needs

Technical need

The technical need for colours can be determined by asking 'can the food be produced without adding colour?'. In most instances the answer is 'yes', since colour does not affect the nutritional qualities of the food. However, if the product is to look sufficiently attractive to gain people's acceptance and if they will not purchase a product without added colour, it can be deemed to be necessary. Colour is also needed in products such as sweets or instant desserts for which there is a demand but which would not exist or would be uneconomic to produce without added colour.

Technical need may be claimed by manufacturers for one or more of the following reasons.

Making food more attractive

Colour may be used for purely decorative purposes, for example on an iced cake, in boxed chocolates or in a layered trifle. Although the product does not need colour to taste and look acceptable, the colour enhances the appearance and hence the quality, so is considered technically necessary.

Colour may also be used to differentiate between products, for example in red Leicester cheese where annatto or beta-carotene

(E160) is used to give an orange colour, and in sage Derby where green colour is added to heighten the appearance and make it look as though the herb has been dispersed through the cheese.

Colour association

Some products would cease to exist in the form in which they are known without the addition of colour. The colour is not technically essential, but has become associated with certain products – dandelion and burdock pop, iced lollies and jellies depend on the mixture of colour and flavour added to them.

Reinforcing weak colours

The technical need to reinforce colour naturally present in ingredients is perhaps less strong now than in the past. Previously, for example, it was thought necessary to colour the fruits added to yoghurts so that they could be seen. Caramel colouring was widely used to strengthen the colour in brown bread but has now been shown to be unnecessary, and removed from most varieties. The addition of colour to some orange and lemon drinks would also come in this category, since they are naturally quite pale. As consumers have shown a willingness to accept products with less colour, the case for a need to reinforce it has diminished, and may even disappear.

Replacing colour

Heat treatment destroys natural colour, and some manufacturers have traditionally replaced it, for example in canned or bottled fruit and vegetables. Apart from loss of colour during heat treatment, sulphur dioxide (E220) acts as a bleaching agent, and further reduces the colour of fruit which has been sulphited for preservation before use in jam. Synthetic dyes have been used in strawberry, raspberry and cherry products and in canned peas to replace the colour lost in processing. There are differences of opinion within the industry, and among consumers, about the extent to which this use of colouring is necessary, and consumers are now able to choose in some shops between coloured and uncoloured varieties.

Natural colours may fade on exposure to light, for example in squashes, salad cream and other products stored in transparent bottles. There may be a technical need to replace the natural colour with one which is not sensitive to light, if the product is to remain attractive over the required shelf-life. Manufacturers also have the option of using coloured or opaque packaging to reduce the exposure, and this is now being done, for example with fresh green pasta.

Consistency

Consumers have become used to products with consistent colour – this creates a technical need for it to be added to some foods. Many of the natural colours vary in intensity at different times of the year, or when obtained from different sources. Some do not mix well, and this can result in 'spotting' or patchiness in the food. The use of synthetic additives enables the final colour of the product to be strictly controlled. Research continues to try to improve the quality of the natural colours which are increasingly demanded.

Deception?

Added colour is used by some manufacturers to make products appear like an alternative. Hence, some 'roast' chickens, for example, are steam-cooked before being flash-roasted to give the appearance of roasting. Others have their skins coloured with brown FK (154) to make them look as if they have been roasted.

Increasingly, manufacturers are using extenders, proteins and bulking agents in products. These affect texture, but may also be uninspiring in colour. The addition of colour, for example to a meat pie or vegetarian sauce, may therefore make it more appetising. It may also imply, however, that different ingredients have been used to those which are present. Red colouring in tomato-flavour pastes, or pink in a strawberry flavour yoghurt, show that people need to pay close attention to the content if they are not to be misled about quality.

The technical need for a colour is largely dependent on the quality of the ingredients and the processing methods used. The technical need to add colour diminishes when foods are packaged in light-proof containers, if freezing is used rather than canning, and if sulphiting agents are removed.

Where a similar colour is technically unsuitable

Not all colours can be used for all purposes. For example, in products which are to be heat-treated, such as a fruit purée or soup, any added colour must remain stable when heated, but most of the natural colours are not heat-stable.

Anthocyanins, which are often used to colour things red, turn blue in an acid medium, and so their use in drinks is limited, such as in flavoured milks.

Copper chlorophyll (E141) is used in table jellies, some lemon and lime squashes, and in green sweets, as the natural green is unsuitable because it fades on exposure to light. Some cola manufacturers argue that there is no suitable substitute for ammonia caramel if the present colour and flavour is to be retained. Yet malt extract is being used successfully by some companies in cola drinks, as well as in meat sauces and vinegar.

Economic need

Perhaps surprisingly, colours appear about halfway down tables showing the tonnage and market value of food additives in the UK. They are substantially exceeded both in quantity and value by flavours, thickeners, stabilisers, emulsifiers and acids. Even so, in 1984 it was estimated that 9000 tonnes of colouring were sold, with a market value of £12 million a year.

Manufacturers would not have replaced synthetic colours with more expensive natural ones unless they were able to recoup or absorb the additional cost. Companies which felt that there was a commercial risk in excluding colours have, on the whole, retained them. Although some have stopped selling certain products for which a satisfactory colour could not be achieved without compromising their policy on the use of additives, none expressed the view to us that this was detrimental to their economic interests. Some companies try to formulate their products so that they are acceptable internationally and they claim that the trend towards using natural colours has been advantageous.

Safety factors

The safety of food colours has received more public attention in recent years than the safety of any other group of additives.

Too much colour?

In 1979 the FAC considered figures showing estimated amounts of colour which people might consume as part of their normal diet. The Committee stated: 'On the whole we found the estimates of colour intakes . . . very reassuring.' Every effort was made to ensure that the levels of consumption were not under-estimated, yet 'the probable daily intake of almost every colour was well within the respective acceptable daily intake'. However, in the case of a child's diet, the estimated intake of several colours was close to, or marginally exceeded, acceptable levels.

Patterns of consumption and additive use have changed significantly since that report was published, and it is not possible to draw conclusions based on those figures. In the UK, the lack of monitoring of total food and additive consumption patterns means that assessments are not kept up to date. The change from synthetic to natural colours may have increased the quantities of colour consumed, since natural colours have to be used in higher concentrations to achieve the same effect as synthetics. Since the number of colours is now more limited, and manufacturers are relying more heavily on certain colours, people are likely to eat more of each individual one. But this may be balanced by the removal of colour from several foods which will have reduced consumption by some people. In short, we don't know how much people are eating. The FAC has now asked for revised data to be produced.

The FAC is particularly concerned that we may all be eating too much caramel. It is thought that this one colour may account for 98 per cent of the colouring which most of us eat in any year. The Committee believes that the levels are too high, and has recommended that caramel be banned in those products in which it is not currently used, and that the quantity which can be added to individual foods be limited. Although there is no clear evidence of damage to health, the main concerns are that:

- many different types of caramel are on sale – it can be made by burning sugar, as you could do at home, but is more commonly made by heating carbohydrates with ammonia and sulphur dioxide. But you won't be able to tell which type of colouring has been used since both types of caramel are labelled in the same way
- the specifications for many of these types of caramel are not standard, so it is not possible to relate safety data for one sort of caramel to another
- the tests which have been done suggest that some types of caramel may be toxic at certain levels and should therefore be limited.

Certain manufacturers, particularly brewers, who use substantial quantities of caramel in dark beers, and the makers of liquorice sweets, in which high concentrations are used, are fervently opposing the proposed limits which they claim will make it impossible for them to produce the products to which people have become accustomed.

Risks of cancer and other toxic effects

Some experts claim that the azo dyes are potentially carcinogenic and are the most suspect group of all food additives. Others feel equally strongly that the arguments have been exaggerated, that the results of some experiments are inconclusive, or that it is possible to establish 'no effect levels' on the basis of animal experiments (in other words, in quantities that someone could be expected to consume, a particular additive would have no effect on his or her health). Those who endorse the latter view consider that the evidence is sufficient to ensure the safety of particular additives in certain foods and that these should continue to be permitted.

Allegations have been made that the colours listed below may either produce carcinogenic reactions or cause toxic effects in animal experiments. All are currently permitted for use in the UK. (Yellow 2G, already accepted as toxic, is not discussed because the Government has issued draft regulations with the intention that it be banned in the near future.)

Amaranth (E123) This has been a controversial colour since it was banned both in the USSR and the USA on the basis of a Soviet study which showed carcinogenic effects in long-term tests on rats, mice and dogs. Some but not all studies suggest that cells exposed to amaranth can mutate, an indication that the substance may be cancer-inducing. In the USA, toxic effects were identified in one in ten studies, although the Food and Drug Administration subsequently stated that amaranth has not been shown to be a carcinogen, and that their research did not confirm other evidence that it could put a foetus at risk.

Differing views remain. As a result, in 1979 the COT classified it in Group 'B' and asked for long-term and carcinogenicity studies to be set up. In 1983 the SCF gave it only temporary approval. However, as additional research has become available, the safety assessment has become more favourable. In 1987 the COT took account of recent studies in rats which did not show any carcinogenic effects, and the toxic effects identified were thought to be part of the rats' natural ageing process. It has now been included in group 'A'.

Brown FK (154) Studies considered by the COT in 1979 showed that it might cause cancer in that it could cause cells to mutate. This may indicate that future generations could be at risk or that cancer cells may form. In 1987, however, a more up-to-date rat study showed no evidence of carcinogenicity and, on the contrary, rats fed brown FK showed a reduced risk of cancer. Studies on several generations of rats showed no effects on reproduction. Nevertheless, the FAC proposes that its use be limited to colouring kippers and marking meat.

Brown HT (155) Although it has been shown as likely to cause cancer at high dose levels in rats, 'no-effect levels' have been identified. The FAC considers that brown HT is safe, given low levels of consumption by humans, and subject to maximum levels of use in food.

Erythrosine (E127) This colour remains controversial, despite the FAC's recommendation in 1987 that it continue to be permitted for limited use in colouring cherries. Carcinogenic effects on the thyroid of rats have been recorded in a number of studies. The COT concluded that at the levels currently consumed in a normal human diet, erythrosine posed no risk of thyroid cancer. Human studies with low levels of erythrosine showed no effect on the thyroid, but the FAC has nevertheless recommended that consumption be kept to very low levels by restricting its use to glacé and cocktail cherries. It may currently be consumed in undesirable amounts in biscuits, sweets and cherry products.

Red 2G (128) Mutations have been recorded at high levels of use in animal experiments, and some concern has been expressed about effects on people with an enzyme deficiency in red blood cells. The COT said that the problems should not occur at low levels of consumption, and the FAC has now recommended that it be permitted only in meat products and vegetable protein meat substitutes.

Adverse reactions

Some food colours have been associated with adverse reactions. The Ministry of Agriculture, Fisheries and Food (MAFF) has consistently maintained that the number of people at risk is low, and that the size of the problem has been exaggerated. Recent research appears to confirm that view (see Chapter 2). Nevertheless, those people who are at risk from adverse reactions may react to certain colours.

Although it is tartrazine that has received the most attention, all the azo dyes are similar in structure, and anyone who exhibits a reaction to one could also develop symptoms from another.

Recent research, funded by MAFF, which looked at the effects of high levels of tartrazine on normal (ie non-intolerant) adults showed that in nine out of ten cases, levels of histamine in the blood were increased. (Histamine is released in allergic-type responses, and can cause a variety of unpleasant symptoms.) In tests using carmoisine, a similar chemical, however, additional histamine was not released: even at twenty times the estimated average intake of tartrazine, no symptoms appeared in the individuals tested.

People who experience adverse reactions to tartrazine may develop asthma, migraine, dermatitis, rashes and other skin complaints. Sunset yellow, in small amounts below those normally found in food, can induce nettlerash in people who suffer adverse reactions. Other studies have shown that brilliant blue FCF, ponceau 4R, patent blue V, quinoline yellow, indigo carmine, erythrosine and amaranth can also cause adverse reactions, usually in those people who also react to other foods or aspirin. A recent study in High Wycombe showed that a child's mood changed after testing with a mixture of azo colours. Why this can happen is not yet clear.

An EEC committee which studied the incidence of adverse reactions in 1980 noted that among people who were sensitive to additives, the incidence of a reaction to tartrazine was very variable, but higher than that for azo dyes in general. It is not clear whether children are at any more risk than the population as a whole.

Evidence from the United States that a diet free from artificial food colours and flavours produced a rapid and dramatic improvement in 25–50 per cent of hyperactive children has been received with some scepticism in official circles in the UK. Some doctors continue to question whether food colours are capable of inducing hyperactivity in children who did not previously react adversely to anything or merely of provoking the reaction in those who have already experienced reactions.

While noting the continuing concern among the general public, the COT commented in 1987 that a variety of natural food ingredients are also capable of causing adverse reactions, and that new evidence was beginning to cast doubt on the general validity of the association between adverse reactions to aspirin and tartrazine. The FAC stated at the same time that none of the reports in recent years would lead it to conclude that the problem of adverse reactions to azo dyes is common, although it wished to see more reliable estimates.

Synthetic colours are not alone in causing reactions. Annatto can provoke symptoms in individuals who already have adverse reactions to other foods. It is possible that the increasing use of natural substances to colour foods may merely shift the problem of adverse reactions from one group of people to another.

Additives about which too little is known

For some colours, such as caramel, curcumin and turmeric, there has been insufficient data for their safety to be assessed, and while the COT does not consider them to present any risk, they have been on the 'B' list pending additional information for many years.

Adverse data exist on the **ammonia caramels** (E150) (as opposed to burnt sugar caramels), and the concern relates to the possible presence of impurities. But since there is no evidence that they are cancer-inducing and since no other effects on people have been recorded, the SCF concluded that ammonia caramels could continue to be used pending further information. Yet although a level at which there was no effect on animals was established, the SCF agreed a safety factor of 10 rather than the usual 100 for calculating the acceptable daily intake. Even with this reduced safety factor, brown beer drinkers would reach the acceptable limit when drinking seven litres in one day. Since this margin of safety was not considered sufficient, the SCF proposed further limits on the presence of impurities. Someone who drinks a great deal of beer or stout could still consume more than the acceptable daily intake.

The FAC is not worried enough to recommend a ban but thinks that since ammonia sulphite caramels are widely used in cola drinks consumed by children there is an urgent need for the safety of these colours to be established or their use prohibited. Human tests using double the normal quantities gave rise to gastro-intestinal problems; results of carcinogenicity tests for ammonia sulphite caramels are not yet available. The COT considers that these issues should be resolved urgently and some consumer groups have suggested that ammonia caramels should be banned until their safety can be assured. Maybe a new name should be found for these or for the burnt sugar caramels so that people can distinguish between the two types.

Lack of information on **carbon black** (E153) has prevented an acceptable daily intake being set. The COT considered it in 1979, and noted that preparations from vegetable sources only would meet the specifications for a food grade product. Although information was lacking, vegetable carbon was considered acceptable for use, on the basis that it was already being used for medicinal purposes without adverse effects. It was not reviewed in the 1987 study, however.

Although some studies on **indigo carmine (E132)** were considered to be below present day standards, the COT was satisfied in 1979 that there was sufficient evidence to allow its use to continue, and did not review the colour again in 1987.

Are natural colours safer?

There is virtually no basis for claiming that a natural colour is any safer than an artificial one. All additives must be toxicologically tested before safety can be assessed. In practice, not all the naturally occurring colours have been fully evaluated, although they have all been reviewed by the COT before being authorised for use. Information on beet red (E162), for example, which is increasingly used, is limited, so no acceptable daily intake has been set.

The COT recommended in 1987 that one form of annatto, capsorubin (E160c – the natural colour in paprika), paprika itself, crocin and santalin (the colours in saffron and sandalwood) be removed from the permitted list because there is insufficient information to assess their safety. No decision has yet been made by the Government.

Changes in the pipeline

In 1987 the FAC completed a comprehensive review of permitted colours. The Committee has accepted in principle that there is a need for food to continue to be coloured if consumers are to have an adequate and varied diet, attractively presented. The addition of substances for no nutritional purpose, just to colour foods, should, it considers, be scrutinised, except for those products (such as sweets and ice lollies) which it accepts would otherwise be completely colourless. The Committee has recommended maximum levels of use for all the colours used in foods, and that certain natural colours, for which insufficient safety information is available, be banned. It also proposes to rectify an anomalous situation whereby if colour is used in the feed of chickens or fish to colour the eggs or flesh, its use does not currently need to be declared when the foods are sold.

The stricter controls proposed, if implemented by Ministers, would ensure that the use of colours did not continue to grow unquestioned. Furthermore, by recommending that certain natural colours be banned, the FAC is also underlining the importance of full evaluation of all additives (whatever their origin) before they are permitted in food.

The UK not only permits more colours to be used than almost any other country but permits them in a wider range of products than some countries would allow. Hence, amaranth, allowed in the UK for use in any food, may be found in packet foods, sauces, tinned fruit, jam, ice-cream, cake mixes, biscuits and yoghurt, whereas in France and Italy it is permitted only in caviare. More than 50 colours are permitted for use in the UK, compared with 32 in Austria and 19 in Norway. France does not permit colours to be added to meat products or to most canned fruit and vegetables. Austria and Sweden do not permit added colour in any meat products, bread, fruit juices or single-fruit jams.

There may well be scope for further limiting the range of foods to which colour may be added. In 1987, MAFF published a *Survey of colour usage in food*. This showed that the most widely used colour was tartrazine, which was recorded in 2,295 products. Caramels came next, being used in 1,221 products but at much higher levels, with sunset yellow close behind (1,215 examples). The naturally occurring colours were less frequently used, but of these the most common were annatto (in the forms of bixin/norbixin) contained in 129 products, carotene in 118 and curcumin in 76.

By recommending a limit on the quantities of colour which can be used in food, and a ban on the addition of colour to foods in which they are not currently used, the Committee has taken a stronger line than in the past. Some consumer groups, however, regret that there has been no attempt to ban the use of colour in those products which it has proved possible to produce without any added colour, such as yoghurt, pre-packed soft drinks for immediate consumption, and canned fruit and vegetables.

It is also thought undesirable for colour to be allowed to mislead people over the quality of products such as pies, sausages or ready meals, and it may benefit consumers if the range of foods to which colour may be added was further restricted. For example, colour is rarely added to wholemeal bread and breakfast cereals, but these do not appear on the list of products which the FAC recommends in future should not be coloured.

The FAC concluded: 'Consumer tastes are, in general, best catered for by the law of supply and demand operating in a free market. In such a market, it should be possible for both coloured and uncoloured foods to be produced and sold', but people should be given sufficient information to exercise an informed choice.

The safety assessment of certain colours continues to raise questions in people's minds. Despite the adverse reports on erythrosine, red 2G and brown FK, these colours will continue to be permitted, albeit for limited purposes in small quantities in individual products. No restrictions have been proposed on those colours which have been associated with adverse reactions: the official position is to support better labelling so that the small proportion of the population at risk may identify foods to avoid. This position is less restrictive than in Norway where all synthetic colours are banned. The continued preference of consumers for natural alternatives may in the long term, however, reduce demand for some synthetic colours to the point where they would be uneconomic anyway.

While use of colours, and in particular the amounts which can be used, will be more tightly controlled if the FAC recommendations are put into practice by the Government, ultimately the choice whether or not to colour a product rests with the manufacturers. If they choose not to colour a product, a number of options of how to achieve the same effects are open to them. They may decide to increase the quantities of particular ingredients, so that for example, more, or higher quality, meat removes the need for colour in pies or sausages. They may boost the natural colour contained in a squash or yoghurt, say, to a level where it is considered satisfactory, by increasing the quantities of fruit. These options are likely to increase the cost in most instances.

Another possibility is to alter the means of processing so that the addition of colour is unnecessary. For example, quick-freezing vegetables or sausages preserves natural colour, whereas bottling or canning destroys it.

Or they may choose an artificial or a natural additive: that choice will depend on the policy of the company, the processing of the product being made, and the range of colours available which are technically capable of achieving the effect. One company told us that the 'removal of colour from pork pie fillings has detracted from the attractive appearance', but they continue to find a market for it; Melton Mowbray pies have traditionally not contained colour.

Manufacturers identify different markets for different quality products and that affects their choice and use of colour. One mint sauce manufacturer commented, for example, that their own-brand mint sauce uses natural colourings while those made for retailers' own-labels uses artificial!

As long as colours are widely permitted in most foods, manufacturers will choose which products are coloured, and the type and quantity of colour used. Consumers will have to exercise their power in the market place to show whether they are willing to continue to buy products in which colour has, in their view, been unnecessarily used. They will themselves determine whether the existence of the technical need to make a product more appealing justifies its indefinite use.

Action points

Added colour is necessary only for aesthetic purposes, so it should always be possible to avoid those products which contain it by picking foods which are not processed and varieties of foods which have not been coloured.

If you want to avoid colours about which there are unresolved

*safety questions or which have been associated with adverse
reactions in some people, look out for the following:*

Annatto *Margarine, low-fat spreads, cheeses, salad cream and
mayonnaise, custards, sponge cakes, ice-cream, ice lollies,
cole-slaw, pastry, soft drinks, liqueurs.*

Azo and other artificial dyes *(tartrazine, yellow 2G, sunset
yellow FCF, quinoline yellow, carmoisine, amaranth,
erythrosine, ponceau 4R, patent blue V, red 2G, indigo carmine,
brilliant blue FCF, brown FK, chocolate brown HT, black PN,
pigment rubine) Biscuits, bread crumb coatings, sweets, dessert
mixes, frozen and ready-made desserts, ice-cream and lollies,
cakes, jellies, preserves, sauces, pickles, mustard, soups,
soft drinks, yoghurts, fillings and toppings, custard.*

Brown FK *Kippers, smoked mackerel, some crisps, the skin of
cooked chicken.*

Brown HT *Imitation chocolate products, preserves, pickles and
some soft drinks.*

Caramel *Beer, some other alcoholic drinks, cola drinks, biscuits,
chocolates, dessert mixes, bread, crisps, meat products, prepared
meals, pickles, sauces, soups, preserves, sweets.*

Erythrosine *Canned cherries, strawberries and rhubarb,
products which contain cherries such as cakes and biscuits,
chocolates, and glacé cherries themselves; garlic sausage,
luncheon meat, salami, salmon spread, pâté, Scotch eggs.*

Red 2G *Sausages, cooked meats, meat pies, frozen meals.*

5
Full of flavour

The background

Flavourings are the largest group of additives. More than 3,500 have been recorded, but the number is increasing all the time. The flavour industry is creative, and highly responsive to demand. Specialised flavours are developed to meet the particular needs of companies for different types of flavour for different products, or for a flavour with particular properties – a liquid, or a powder, or one which will dissolve in acid. Many companies have individual specifications for their strawberry, hazelnut or coffee flavours, for example. People's demand for more 'natural' flavours has been reflected by manufacturers and over the years, as flavour extraction methods have improved, better and more realistic flavours have been obtained.

Types of flavour

As with colours, flavours may be natural, nature-identical or artificial. Natural flavours are obtained from plant sources such as leeks, oranges, lemons and nuts. To be called 'natural' they must be processed using exclusively physical procedures such as pressing, distilling or concentrating.

Many flavours originate from sources which most people would not consider edible, although flavour chemists classify them as natural. An extensive list prepared by the FAC in 1976 included acacia, white poplar, cinnamon, cinchona and other tropical trees; leaves from the cranberry, bilberry and cherry; a number of wild flowers such as violets, speedwell and red clover; and the herbs and spices which might be used at home.

Given the choice, would you be happy that Eastern hemlock, prickly ash or ground ivy had gone into your food? All are potential sources of flavour. Deadly nightshade, lily of the valley and slippery elm have also been used as flavours, although they are thought to be toxic.

Of the other two groups of flavours, nature-identical substances are synthetically produced, but are chemically identical with the flavouring compounds found naturally in foods. Synthetic flavours are obtained by chemical production from compounds which are not known to exist in nature.

Flavour enhancers have little or no flavour themselves, but intensify, strengthen or alter the flavour or smell of other substances. Garlic and onions naturally have this property, but the most common flavour enhancer is monosodium glutamate – MSG (621). It can be made from seaweed, but is more usually produced from sugar beet or wheat. It stimulates the tastebuds and is used in sauces, stocks, soups, pork pies, sausages, delicatessen meats and convenience foods, and can also be bought for home use. Other permitted enhancers include guanosine 5'-(disodium phosphate) (627), inosine 5'-(disodium phosphate) (631) and sodium 5'-ribonucleotide (635). They are most commonly found in products which have been dehydrated (such as crisps and snacks), slow-frozen (such as potato products), or heat-preserved (such as flavoured rice): all these processes cause products to lose their flavour. Ribonucleotides (635) are effective in salty products, and unlike MSG may be used in egg and pickle products. Some are also used in cooked, cured meats.

Other sources of flavour

Some manufacturers use acids to help create a sharp or sour taste, especially if they are already being used for other functions in the product, for example as preservatives, to dissolve food colours, or to adjust acidity. Citric acid (E330) is the most commonly used, and occurs naturally in citrus fruit. It is commercially prepared from the fermentation of molasses, and is used as a flavouring agent in soft drinks, tinned fruit, sauces, ice-cream, jam, jellies, frozen chips and confectionery.

Hydrolysed vegetable protein (HVP) has been used as a meat flavour and flavour enhancer since the beginning of this century, and was originally a by-product of MSG manufacture – it has a high MSG content. It is heat-stable and is used in canned foods. MSG has been associated with adverse reactions in some people, and the consumer resistance arising from this has increased manufacturers' dependence on HVP. Since hydrolysed vegetable protein can be labelled as an ingredient, not an additive, it has a marketing advantage over MSG – people may wrongly believe that they are getting a product with fewer additives and no MSG, when that is not the case. Other natural proteins are also being developed to give a meaty flavour, so MSG quantities can be reduced or eliminated in the future.

Consumers' needs

It is particularly difficult to define the need for flavours, although they are central features of modern food processing. Flavours are not 'needed' in the sense that they are not a source of nutrients, but by adding taste they may enhance the acceptability of food. The question is, do people want the flavours used? If not, would there still be a sufficient range of products to offer them a choice?

Choice and variety

Henry Heath, doyen of the flavouring industry, has said: 'There can be no one who has any doubts of the prime importance of odour and flavour in making our diet interestingly appetising, irrespective of its nutritional value.' Herein lies the heart of the debate about the need for flavour – people clearly want food which is varied in taste, and of acceptable quality. Without added flavour certain foods, such as soft drinks and confectionery, would be quite tasteless and the range of foods such as ice-cream, desserts and snacks would be limited. Some people would question the use, for example, of flavours in yoghurts or soft drinks, in place of fruit. But are such products 'inferior' or merely 'different'?

Flavour plays a key role in determining the perceived quality of many foods. People closely associate taste, smell and colour in food, and they can be misled about the quality of a product by the sophisticated use of flavour. For example, incorporating a cheese flavour into a vegetable substitute which looks like cheese on a pizza may lead some consumers to believe real cheese has been used. Labelling of flavours is not yet sufficiently clear to ensure that people know the real content (see Chapter 3).

The replacement of some ingredients with added flavour may widen choice and permit the sale of cheaper alternatives, but people should at least know what they are buying, and have the choice of foods without added flavour, if that is what they want. And, when a flavouring agent has been used in place of the 'real thing', the labelling should make this plain.

No objective tests have tried to determine the extent of demand for the variety of flavours which exist. No-one appears to have questioned as a matter of principle whether, and to what extent, flavours should continue to be used. Only if consumers themselves demand that the range be limited will the rate of development of exotic and improved flavours slow down. At present there seems to be little evidence that this is what consumers want. There appears to be no limit to the inventiveness of flavourists, who try to meet what they consider to be the demand for an unlimited range of products – they may yet produce flavours for savoury yoghurts, coffee-flavoured soft drinks . . .

Natural or synthetic?

In recent years consumers have expressed a clear choice for 'natural' rather than 'synthetic' flavours, as part of the wider demand for more 'natural' foods. The industry has responded with an increasing variety of flavours for different foods. Mineral waters, for example, may not by law contain any additives, and yet flavoured mineral waters are now on sale, governed by the regulations on soft drinks. One supplier of French mineral water commented that the company uses only natural flavours derived from the essence of organically grown fruit.

Most high street retailers have also responded to pressure to change as far as their own-brand products are concerned. They recognise the marketing advantage from describing additives as 'natural', but differ in their definitions so that some include 'nature-identical' as natural, while others consider them to be 'artificial'. Without knowledge of the actual flavour sources, it is impossible to tell from the label which approach has been used.

Consumers may well question many of the substances described as 'natural' when used to flavour food. They are not, in most cases, foods in themselves, and the flavour added is not 'natural' in many instances to the product in which it is used, as for example with fruit- or nut-flavoured yoghurts. Many people now believe that flavours which are not from a known, edible source should be described as 'artificial' – this approach is followed in the labelling laws of some countries.

Manufacturers' needs

Technical need

People have flavoured and spiced their food for thousands of years so it is no surprise that manufacturers also use flavours to modify the taste and smell of food. They express the need for flavours to accomplish the following tasks:

- to restore flavour lost in processing. Cooking (particularly at high temperatures) and preservation destroy flavours such as those in fruit and vegetable products, especially where the original flavour was not strong
- to reinforce naturally weak flavours. Meat flavours are especially mild and may need enhancement, as for example in some low-fat sausages. Many natural fruit flavours would be required in very high concentrations to create the intensity of flavour achieved using only a small amount of an artificial substitute
- to improve the palatability of bland products, such as rice or soya protein, to give flavour to products such as confectionery and soft drinks, and to extend choice of biscuits, savoury snacks and crisps and so on
- to provide a consistent flavour where the natural one would vary in strength from batch to batch
- to replace a more expensive process – such as dipping products in smoke solution rather than smoking cheeses or

fish products, or to reduce the quantity of major ingredients while maintaining an acceptable flavour, for instance the quantity of meat in pies or sausages.

In practice, some retailers are attempting to replace flavours and flavour enhancers with herbs, spices or other alternative ingredients. These highly successful changes raise two questions: how much did they need these additives in the first place, and should other manufacturers continue to claim that they still need them? A pasta company, whose policy is not to use food additives if they can be avoided, is currently undertaking trials with various seasonings in ravioli. One retailer has managed to remove MSG and all artificial flavours from its own brand foods, but has found that this limits choice considerably. Cheese and onion, an artificial flavour used in crisps, has been replaced with spring onion. Vinegar and chilli flavours for crisps are also available from natural sources.

One frozen food retailer commented to us that taking MSG out of products has had no perceivable effect, although in some products the salt content has been increased to compensate, or herbs and spices added. The company has removed MSG from all sausages and meat products where it was used, and where the taste differs, the product is not considered any less acceptable. Where the product without MSG was unsatisfactory, the company has stopped selling it. This is a minority view: most retailers do not question the use of MSG, or consider it essential in the products in which it is used.

On the other hand, the flavour-making industry has itself been highly critical of manufacturers' demand for natural flavours. They stress, in particular, the variation in the quality and strength of flavour, insecurity of supply of the raw materials, the possibility of bacterial contamination, the higher concentrations required to achieve a satisfactory taste, and in particular the limitations that this will place on choice of flavours in foods. Indeed, one flavour industry spokesman has gone so far as to suggest that 'with the current interest in conservation and with increasing world population, we should, wherever possible, avoid destruction of good natural foodstuff just to produce flavourings for convenience products . . . We should keep and enjoy a field of fresh strawberries and use nature-identical flavours for manufactured products.'

In fact, the emphasis in research is on developing nature-identical varieties. They are cheaper, more consistent, more concentrated and more convenient to use than the corresponding natural flavours. They can be used in very small quantities, have precise specifications and are not subject to the variation in quality which affects natural alternatives.

Economic need

Flavours are the largest sector of the additives market, in both tonnage and volume. The London Food Commission estimated that in 1984 the total UK market for flavours was worth £65 – £70 million and that it would grow at 4–5 per cent a year over the next few years.

In a highly competitive industry, keeping down costs while maintaining sales is essential for survival. Even though manufacturers might acknowledge that the most wholesome products would include natural ingredients such as meat extracts, cheese or vegetable products, substitution of flavours for ingredients is one of the easiest ways for them to reduce costs. So, for example, imitation tomato flavourings, pastes and extenders have found a substantial market, and the use of enzyme-modified cheese flavours can allow up to 50 per cent of the cheese to be replaced with only a small amount of flavour. The use of meat extracts has declined over recent years as they are now relatively expensive, and other meat flavours are being substituted.

Undoubtedly when raw material costs increase, manufacturers may feel under pressure to lower the quality of some products in order to maintain their position in the market. If the composition of a product is changed so that its nutritional quality is reduced, consumers must be made aware of the change, so they can make true comparisons of cost and quality between brands.

Safety considerations

Flavours

Assessing the safety of flavours is fraught with difficulty not only because of the vast numbers in use, but also because flavour companies are intensely secretive about the composition of the flavours they produce, and have hindered attempts publicly to assess their safety.

The industry claims that all flavours are assessed by the manufacturers in order to comply with the general requirements of the Food Act, but the evaluations are secret, subject to scrutiny neither by independent scientists nor the public.

One justification put forward as to why flavours are not systematically assessed for safety is that they are used in such small quantities that they cannot pose much risk. Most are used in small amounts but the total quantities consumed are increasing, and natural flavours are used at much higher concentrations than the synthetic varieties. Some, such as ethyl vanillin, are very widely used so levels of consumption could be significant.

Manufacturers recognise the need for all new artificial flavours to be tested before being put on the market, but argue that for some, the costs of development and safety testing are so high compared with the size of the market that production would become uneconomic. Maybe this merely indicates saturation of the flavours market, which could be overcome by producing fewer flavours and testing them thoroughly.

As long ago as 1965, the FAC concluded that 16 flavours should be banned as they were suspected of being harmful. Ministers did not endorse this suggestion. So far nothing has been done, and discussions within the EEC are progressing slowly. There is no way of knowing whether any of the substances which the FAC or the EEC proposed should be banned are still in use: since labels are required only to identify the presence of flavour, but neither the source material nor the actual name, people cannot identify what has been used.

Such inadequate labelling also makes it very difficult to identify adverse reactions to flavouring agents. Adverse reactions to flavouring sources are known in people working in food processing plants, and some common flavours such as cheese and onion or salt and vinegar in crisps have given rise to symptoms among food workers, so it is possible that they may also have an effect on others when eaten.

Flavour enhancers

In the UK, flavour enhancers are regulated and so have been subjected to a more detailed toxicological evaluation than flavours. MSG has been associated with reproductive hazards: changes in the nervous system have been observed in new-born animals given large doses of MSG. For this reason, as a precautionary measure, some flavour enhancers may not be used in foods intended for babies and young children: sodium hydrogen L-glutamate (MSG – 621); guanosine 5'-(disodium phosphate) (627); inosine 5'-(disodium phosphate) (631); sodium 5'-ribonucleotide (635). People suffering from gout and conditions which require them to avoid purines are recommended to avoid guanosine, inosine and riboneucleotides.

When used as a condiment, and eaten on an empty stomach, MSG can produce a condition known as 'Chinese Restaurant Syndrome' in some people. The symptoms include burning sensations in the mouth and throat, palpitations, headache, drowsiness, muscle tightening, nausea and chest pain. Characteristically, symptoms appear about 15–20 minutes after the person has eaten a lot of oriental food in a restaurant and last up to a few hours. Attacks can be mild or moderately severe. Reactions to packaged food seem rare – the condition seems to result from using MSG like salt in the kitchen or at table, and is rare.

A framework for future control

For more than 20 years unsuccessful attempts have been made to regulate the use of flavours in Britain. Flavour companies shroud their products in secrecy which is quite out of keeping both with modern food legislation, and the consumer's desire to know what has gone into the food he or she eats. Even retailers find it difficult to obtain precise specifications for the flavours used in their products. Some big retailers insist on it, but others have less power to demand the information. One retailer told us that to gain information on the flavours used in ingredients they may have to approach several different companies. Where products are imported, or contain imported ingredients, the suppliers may not themselves know what has been used.

One retailer expressed the view that 'commercial sensitivity in this area is nothing more than a sacred cow which has built up over the years'. All companies supplying own-brand goods are required to divulge the recipes and contents to the firm for which they made the food. Some of those retailers whom we interviewed saw no reason to treat flavours differently from other additives. They believed that the public had no confidence in the flavour manufacturers' ability to regulate their own industry, and that without Government control consumers would not be able to gain information to which they have a right and which might be significant for health. Others supported the flavour manufacturers and thought that self-regulation would be sufficient.

Consumer organisations are united in their view that all flavours should be properly tested and products clearly labelled so that consumers can identify the contents. They question the validity of treating flavours differently from other additives, and regret the considerable delays in agreeing how full safety assessment can best be achieved.

Indeed it has been the failure of public authorities nationally and internationally to agree on how flavours should be controlled which has allowed the industry a free rein for so long. Debate centres not on whether there should be regulations, but on the most appropriate system.

Five different approaches have been suggested:

- the setting up of a permitted list which specifies all the flavours which may be used, as is the case with most other categories of additive in the UK
- the compilation of negative lists which state those substances which should be prohibited, and which by implication permit any other substance. This approach was rejected by UK

Ministers in the 1960s, and continues to be opposed by MAFF who say they would not know which new flavour sources were being isolated and so would not be able to provide adequate protection for consumers

- a combination of both these lists, plus a third one of substances generally thought to be safe but which would be subject to review within a specified time
- the drawing up of mixed lists which would allow almost any natural substances to be used, on the grounds that they are generally recognised as safe, and provided the level of contaminants contained in them is controlled. The lists would also set down a limited number of permitted synthetic flavours but ban any natural and artificial flavours which may pose a health risk
- allowing the free market, and general food law, to continue to operate.

Both the UK Government and the EEC are committed to controlling all additives by means of permitted lists, and in 1980 the EEC issued a proposal which aimed to ensure that only those flavours which had been subjected to independent toxicological evaluation, and were on a permitted list, could be used. The proposal ran into difficulties in the European Parliament, and has not yet been adopted.

There are a few countries in which the use of flavours is already regulated with permitted lists: they include the USA, Japan, Italy and Spain. Germany has a mixed system with a very short list of 17 permitted artificial flavours. Natural and nature-identical flavours are permitted but certain substances such as thujone, saffrole and coumarin are prohibited, and the amount of quinine in soft drinks limited. Most other countries (such as France) require that the flavours used should be safe on toxicological grounds or by virtue of long usage. Some countries also specify the foods which may contain artificial flavours (for instance, Germany and Switzerland).

What has been lacking from much of the debate has been any assessment of what is needed and why, and which flavours people want in different products. The EEC's Consumer Consultative

Committee in 1986 seemed to get nearest to tackling the issue when it said that only those additives which pose no risk to health and which are technically indispensable should be used. If consumers were generally aware of the vast number of non-edible sources from which flavours come, they might have different views on what is acceptable for use in food.

6
Who needs sweetening up?

Natural and artificial sweeteners

Sugar provides energy and adds sweetness but it also can make food more palatable, act as a preservative in jam, fruit purées and sauces, and contribute to the texture of foods.

It comes in a variety of forms. What most people think of as sugar is sucrose, which is extracted from sugar cane or sugar beet and then refined. Other sugars include glucose (dextrose) and fructose, which occur naturally in some fruits, vegetables and honey, and lactose, which is the sugar in milk. Sugar may be naturally present in or added to many processed products. All are classed as food ingredients, not additives.

Artificial sweeteners can be used as alternatives to sugar. Manufacturers have responded to consumers' demands for less sugar and fewer calories by using alternative sweeteners in a wide range of products. Low-sugar fruit spreads are now widely available and canned fruit can be bought in juice as an alternative to syrup. Many yoghurts, not just 'diet' yoghurts, contain sweeteners, as do some of the chilled salads, where they offset the acidity of products such as cole-slaw and potato salad. Sweeteners can also be found in sauces, pickles and chutneys in place of sugar.

There are two main types of sweetener – intense and bulk:

Permitted intense sweeteners
These are many times sweeter weight for weight than sugar, but their calorie content is negligible.

Saccharin About 300 times sweeter than sugar, saccharin can withstand high temperatures, but tends to become bitter with prolonged cooking. Some people also find that it has a slightly bitter after-taste. Saccharin is used in soft drinks, canned fruit and vegetables, sauces, pickles and bakery products. Until recently, it was the only permitted artificial sweetener, and as a result has been the most widely used.

Acesulfame K Between 130 and 200 times sweeter than sugar. Acesulfame K can withstand high temperatures, so is useful in home cooking and in processing food and drink.

Aspartame Also known as 'NutraSweet'. It is 200 times sweeter than sugar but becomes less sweet when stored for long periods or used at high temperatures. Aspartame is much more expensive than saccharin, so it has not entirely replaced it. A combination of aspartame and saccharin is widely used in low-calorie drinks. One retailer told us, however, that in yoghurts the mixture of aspartame and saccharin was being replaced by aspartame on its own, as the taste was thought to be better.

Thaumatin Around 2,500 times sweeter than sugar. Thaumatin is a naturally occurring protein extracted from a West African plant. It produces a delayed sensation of sweetness, and so is not suitable on its own. It is available combined with saccharin in granular form.

The food manufacturing industry has argued successfully that the new sweeteners offer people a more satisfactory taste than saccharin which is known to leave a slightly bitter after-taste in the mouth. However, taste tests carried out by *Which?* magazine in April 1986 were inconclusive: the panel was not able to detect significant differences.

Permitted bulk sweeteners
These are similar in sweetness and contain about the same number of calories as sugar, but their technical characteristics differ.

Hydrogenated glucose syrup Slightly less sweet than sugar, this does not crystallise at high concentrations, so has advantages over glucose and sucrose. It is claimed to be less likely to cause dental decay and is therefore used as an alternative to sorbitol (see below) in sweets, soft drinks and low-calorie products.

Isomalt About half as sweet as sucrose, isomalt is less likely to cause browning on cooked foods. It may be used in confectionery, soft drinks and desserts.

Mannitol (E421) Just over half as sweet as sugar. It can be found naturally in pumpkins, mushrooms, onions, beets, celery and olives. Since it is stable at high temperatures, it is used in the preparation of confectionery, boiled sweets, fondant and other products manufactured by boiling sugar. It can also improve the palatability of cakes, and is used as a dusting agent on sheets of chewing gum.

Sorbitol (E420) About half as sweet as sugar, sorbitol occurs naturally in cherries, plums, pears, apples and berries. It is found in similar processed products to mannitol. Its many uses include industrial baking, improving the 'mouth-feel' of soft drinks, reducing the charring and browning of sausages, lowering the freezing point of soft-scoop ice-cream, altering the rate of crystallisation of sweets and sweetening diabetic foods.

Xylitol This is found in raspberries, yellow plums, endives and lettuces. As sweet as sugar, it has a marked 'mouth-cooling effect'. It is less likely to cause browning in cooked foods, and is preferred by manufacturers to sugar because of its stability at high temperatures.

Different sweeteners affect taste in different ways. Which ones a manufacturer uses will depend on the company's priorities and on which taste is considered more acceptable.

The FAC review

In 1982 the FAC carried out a review of sweeteners, and its recommendations were implemented by regulations in 1983. It recommended that the number of permitted sweeteners be increased, to include all those listed above.

It considered that no one bulk sweetener was ideal for all purposes, and decided that a case of need was established for those currently permitted (except thaumatin which it did not recommend as the COT had insufficient information to assess it; the COT subsequently gave an opinion on thaumatin, and it was included in the regulations, but the information on which the decision was based has not been published). The FAC recommended that permitting acesulfame K and aspartame would give manufacturers a degree of flexibility which they had been denied for many years in the absence of an alternative to saccharin.

Requests for a further 12 substances including cyclamates, lactitol and maltitol which had been reviewed by the SCF for consideration on an EEC permitted list were not agreed.

Having stated that a case of need had been proved for eight of the nine substances listed above, the FAC still recommended that restrictions be maintained on some uses of artificial sweeteners: aspartame, acesulfame K, saccharin and thaumatin are prohibited in ice-cream; only a certain amount of saccharin can be used in soft drinks, although other sweeteners may be used in them without restriction; artificial sweeteners may not go into jams, although thaumatin, aspartame, acesulfame K and saccharin may be used in fruit spreads, and any of the permitted sweeteners may be added to diabetic jams.

Sweeteners may be used in any quantities in other products, subject to good manufacturing practice, except in infant and baby food, or when specifically excluded by a compositional standard, such as for cream, jam and beer. Thus, the UK permits sweeteners to be more extensively used than any other Community country, except Ireland, where no legislation exists and the norm is to permit those which are approved for use in the UK. Holland, Belgium, Luxembourg and Denmark all have limits on the foods in which sweeteners may be used and the quantities permitted. Germany mainly permits their use in dietetic products, and has not agreed to the use of aspartame and acesulfame K. Italy allows sweeteners only in registered dietetic products. France, under a law of 1904, bans the use of sweeteners in processed foods.

Consumers' needs

General population

According to the Royal College of Physicians the consumption of sugar per head in Britain is higher than in most countries. Medical opinion suggests that our sugar consumption should not be increased: sugar contributes to dental disease, and it may play a part in the development of obesity. The National Advisory Committee on Nutrition Education (NACNE) and the British Medical Association, however, have both gone further by recommending that we should actually reduce our annual sugar consumption by half.

Cutting back on sugar may mean adjusting to eating fewer sweet foods, but artificial sweeteners can also play a part by permitting sweet-tasting, low-calorie, low-sugar foods. The public want low-calorie alternatives for sugar, in processed foods, as table-top sweeteners, cooking aids, and in tablet form for addition to tea, coffee and other hot drinks. Artificial sweeteners appeal because they contain few or no calories. They also provide sweetness for diabetics who have to avoid sugar.

Substituting artificial sweeteners for sugar may reduce the incidence of dental decay, but while the SCF considers that the bulk sweeteners don't cause tooth decay, other bodies are more cautious and suggest only that hydrogenated glucose syrup, sorbitol, xylitol and isomalt are less damaging than sugar itself.

There is clearly a demand for artificial sweeteners, but is there really a fundamental need for sweeteners to be added to foods? While contributing to the taste, acceptance and palatability of products, we could, if we chose, manage without them, and adjust our taste for sweet foods by gradually becoming accustomed to less sweet versions. For example, many people find that they can eventually get used to tea or coffee without sugar. Indeed, in the past manufacturers have not asked for artificial sweeteners to be added to baby foods, and the regulations now prohibit it. If babies can do without such sweet foods, why can't children and adults?

Special dietary needs

It is very important to provide a wide range of products that contain alternatives to sugar for diabetics. Diabetics must control their consumption of foods containing rapidly absorbable carbohydrates such as sucrose, because they produce insufficient insulin to deal with the sugar. Certain bulk sweeteners may be used as a replacement since they require less insulin than the equivalent amount of sucrose, and are effective in jams and confectionery which diabetics would otherwise be unable to enjoy freely.

People who are seriously overweight may be advised to reduce their consumption of sugar as part of a calorie-controlled diet, and reduced-calorie products are valuable to them.

Manufacturers' needs

Technical need

Where there is a demand for sweet products which are nevertheless low in calories, artificial sweeteners provide the technical means to achieve it. They are therefore widely used by the food and drink industry.

Alternative sweeteners have to be used if sugar is unsuitable. For example, if sucrose is used to reduce the freezing point of ice-cream, the product tends to develop a grainy or gritty texture and becomes excessively sweet. Water ices containing high levels of sucrose tend to be sticky and suffer from surface crystallisation. Bulk sweeteners such as sorbitol overcome these problems because they do not crystallise so easily, and may be less sweet weight for weight.

For some concentrated soft drinks, it is difficult to provide the necessary degree of sweetness, and at the same time maintain the cloudy nature of the product using just sugar, because some of the constituents separate during storage. This can be prevented by the use of intense sweeteners as a partial substitute for sugar.

Although diabetic foods may be manufactured using bulk sweeteners, since some of these are less sweet than sucrose, additional sweetness may be given by the addition of an intense variety.

The safety of permitted sweeteners

All the sweeteners mentioned above are permitted for use in the UK, although only mannitol and sorbitol also have EEC approval. All have been assessed by the COT. Until recently only acesulfame K had been given the complete approval implied by group 'A' status; the COT said that all the others required further research before being given total clearance. The COT has recently upgraded all the bulk sweeteners to group 'A', but at present no information has been published about the basis on which the decision was made.

The SCF noted that there were problems in carrying out a toxicological evaluation of sweeteners: they are used at comparatively high levels in foods, so cannot be tested at the usual levels in animal experiments (100 times the level of human consumption). Such large quantities might anyway induce toxic effects which would be of doubtful relevance to people. Several of the sweeteners evaluated by the SCF produced unsatisfactory results in animal experiments, although MAFF says that the COT has now been assured of their suitability and safety in use.

Laxative properties

Although isomalt, sorbitol, mannitol and xylitol can produce laxative effects at high doses (10–20 grams per day), the SCF has stated that consumption of 20 grams per day is unlikely to cause undesirable symptoms in most people. The laxative effect depends on the individual sweetener, and whether consumption is spread over a number of meals, or in a large quantity all at once. Personal susceptibility, and whether the person has been fasting, also have an influence but the mechanism is not clear. The SCF found, for example, that children of 2–3 years of age tended to be less susceptible than those aged 5–6 when given the same amount. Sensitive individuals may experience an effect at intakes of 10 grams, while others may tolerate 90 grams without adverse effects. Germany requires warning labels to highlight the laxative properties of sweeteners. The COT is still considering the evidence on laxative properties to see whether any action is necessary in the UK.

It is rare to find isomalt or mannitol in products in the UK – they are more widely used in other parts of the European Community. Sorbitol is the most widely used of the permitted bulk sweeteners in the UK, where it can be found in chocolates, sweets, pastries, ice-creams and diabetic jams.

Adverse reactions

Few of the permitted sweeteners are associated with adverse reactions. Mannitol is known to cause nausea and vomiting but is not as widely used as the others. The COT requested further analysis of a number of effects which were seen in animals tested with mannitol.

In 1986, a letter in the *Lancet* suggested a link between aspartame and epileptic seizures in three previously healthy adults who had consumed large quantities of drinks sweetened with aspartame in the USA. The UK Government was not moved to review the use of aspartame, but commented that epilepsy is a relatively common condition which may affect previously healthy adults of any age.

Cancers

As far as the general population is concerned, the most worrying aspect of any additive is its potential to cause cancer. Although the COT was concerned on this score when it was first considering aspartame, safety levels have now been agreed nationally and internationally.

Saccharin has been the subject of much debate, and a wealth of data confirms that it is responsible for bladder cancer in rats fed high doses. The COT acknowledged these results, but concluded that studies in humans failed to show any link between saccharin and cancer, despite its use over a long period. Although classifying saccharin in Group 'B' (provisionally acceptable for use in food), the COT did not request further information on the mechanism by which the rat tumours were caused, nor whether this would affect people at normal or very high doses. One Canadian research study reckoned that doses of saccharin needed to produce cancer in rats were equivalent to 800 cans of low-calorie drinks per day or 300,000 per year.

While the SCF recommended that the intake of saccharin by children and pregnant women should be limited, and that people should be warned of the risk, the FAC did not adopt this stance. It merely endorsed the view that artificial sweeteners should not be used in food prescribed for babies and young children, but did not recommend additional labelling. In the United States, however, labels are put on products containing saccharin to warn people that 'the use of this product may be hazardous to your health. This product contains saccharin which has been determined to cause cancer in laboratory animals.'

The bulk sweeteners sorbitol, mannitol and xylitol have given the COT cause for concern. When administered at high doses over long periods of time, all gave rise to a range of effects including the formation of bladder tumours in rats. Although the same effects were not seen with isomalt and hydrogenated glucose syrup, the studies available for these did not exceed 90 days. Recent studies considered by JECFA and the COT, however, have suggested that these effects did not result from the sweeteners themselves. The COT has now reclassified the bulk sweeteners as Group 'A' additives and JECFA considers them suitable for unlimited use.

Neurological effects

Aspartame was initially seen as an attractive 'natural' sweetener, because it is made by combining two naturally occurring amino acids, and is digested in the same way as protein, and was thus thought unlikely to cause any problems. However, there is some evidence that aspartame, alone or with glutamate, may contribute to mental retardation, brain damage or neurological conditions. This evidence was not accepted by the COT, since human studies indicated no untoward effects at the levels likely to be used in food and consumed in a normal diet. The COT's decision was also partly based on the fact that aspartame cannot be used in liquids or at high temperatures for technical reasons, so its use was likely to be limited. (The Committee acknowledged that the situation would have to be reviewed if these technological difficulties were overcome.) The SCF also questioned the validity of the results.

Other potentially damaging effects

As we have pointed out, not all the new sweeteners have been fully evaluated for safety, and since many of them are used together some interaction between them is possible. The FAC has asked for further information on the effects of consuming more than one sweetener concurrently compared with equivalent levels of a single sweetener.

Toxicological evaluation is always dependent on levels of consumption. Because it was not known how much the new sweeteners would affect the nation's diet, the FAC recommended that further information on intake in general, and any change in the consumption of saccharin in particular, should be collected within five years. A survey is currently under way to establish the levels of consumption of sweeteners in food by the public and in particular by diabetics. It should be completed in the autumn of 1988. Such information is particularly relevant for children who may be consuming unacceptably high quantities, and for anyone with special dietary needs.

Aspartame contains phenylalanine, which is a potential danger for people with the genetic deficiency that causes phenylketonuria (approximately 1 in 15,000). Their inability to metabolise the amino acid from which aspartame is made may result in its building up in the brain and causing serious damage. Aspartame must be labelled so that those at risk can avoid products containing it. This particular amino acid is also present in milk and chicken, and its presence in aspartame is no cause for general concern.

Action points

Many foods now contain artificial sweeteners to replace natural sugar. The extent to which people need to eat them depends on personal taste, and in principle they are rarely necessary. In practice, many people find that they are a useful aid in maintaining sweetness without calories. Our knowledge of some of the new sweeteners, and particularly the bulk sweeteners, is incomplete. The reasons for adverse results in animal experiments have not been fully or satisfactorily explained, and while the risks to human beings are likely to be low, there may be some effects.

Aspartame *Used in many products, but mainly in soft drinks and low-calorie yoghurt. It may be a problem for people suffering from phenylketonuria, although the sweeteners themselves carry warning labels.*

Saccharin *Used in soft drinks, canned vegetables, bakery products, fruit juice, processed fruit, reduced sugar jams, sauces and many other foods.*

Bulk sweeteners *Used in diabetic foods, sweets, soft drinks, desserts and ice-creams. When consumed in substantial quantities, these can have laxative effects.*

7
The texture modifiers

More than 50 additives are permitted for use as emulsifiers (to mix oil and water together), stabilisers (to stop oils and water separating again), thickeners (to give body and consistency) and gelling agents (to make desserts and jams set). They affect the texture and thickness of foods. One or more of the permitted additives in this group (or modified starch, which is unregulated), are to be found in the majority of processed foods. They are versatile in use – some can also prevent curdling, sticking, crystallisation or caking.

Emulsifiers and stabilisers
These serve several purposes, and individual additives may perform both functions. Emulsifiers and stabilisers are used in products such as margarine, low-fat spreads, mayonnaise and sauces. Ice-cream, dessert mixes, fish products, and cream in aerosol cans may all contain emulsifiers and stabilisers.

Thickeners and gelling agents
These perform similar functions to each other, by thickening a food and improving its consistency. Gelatine, pectin (for jam-making) and starch are well known for their thickening properties and are commonly used at home as well as in the food industry. Vegetable gums act in this way in sauces and pickles, tomato purée, fruit pulp and desserts. Cellulose derivatives are used in fillings for baked products, fish fingers, frozen chips, batter, some cheeses, desserts, sauces and sterilised whipping cream.

The food industry's demand for these additives has mushroomed with the growth in processed food and increased demand for products like ice-cream, confectionery, chocolate, dessert mixes and processed cheeses. But even traditional foods such as bread and cakes may have these additives to 'improve their eating quality' and increase volume.

Have these developments gone too far? Is such extensive use of texture modifiers necessary? The FAC last reviewed the use of emulsifiers and stabilisers in 1970 but since then there has been a vast change in the products in which they appear. Since 1962, the FAC has accepted that 'emulsifiers and stabilisers are necessary, and widely used in the production of bread, flour confectionery, ice-cream, margarine, chocolate and sugar confectionery, some soft drinks and milk products.' It noted that 'in recent years there has been an increase in the number of convenience foods which has been facilitated greatly by the development of new or improved emulsifiers and stabilisers.' There was no reason in principle 'to restrict particular substances once a case of need had been established'. However, certain restrictions were placed on those which could be used in bread, milk, potato products, meat and fish products, ice-cream, baby food and those foods which were significant elements in the diet.

As well as these restrictions, compositional standards for some foods limit the types of emulsifier which can be used (and in some cases the quantity) but the products affected are few. They include cocoa and chocolate products, soft and processed cheese, but these are not essential foods in the diet. Controls on the quantity of thickener that may be used in cream, however, prevent the quality being reduced.

Apart from these limited exceptions, the additives permitted in this group, of which there are nearly sixty, can be used in any foods.

Permitted emulsifiers and stabilisers

Among the permitted additives (of which those with 'E' numbers range from E400–E499) are gums, celluloses, fatty acids and pectin. Starch, one of the main thickeners, is considered to be an ingredient, so while it functions as a thickener it is not required to be declared as such on food labels. Modified starches are starches which have been changed by the use of chemicals, or milled or roasted, to perform better under certain conditions than natural starches. They, too, are labelled as ingredients, although there is pressure for them to be regulated as additives.

Consumers' needs

People's need for these additives has hardly been questioned, so need has mainly been defined by current usage. In 1978, the SCF commented that misuse of texture modifiers could result in excessive water retention in products, with a reduction in the nutritional quality of food. The SCF thought that limits on use should be established and enforced in order to protect consumers. Given that during the past 20 years the range of uses has continued to increase, the time may have come for another review.

Consistency and texture

People have become used to foods of consistent quality and with certain textures. Texture and 'mouth feel' are largely matters of personal preference and are not easily defineable. For example, one retailer recently introduced a range of low-sugar fruit spreads, which require added pectin and gelling agent to achieve a satisfactory set, and stabilisers to prevent the sugars in the fruit separating out. The company was content with the range of jams, but the marmalade texture was found too gelatinous to be satisfactory in taste tests.

Emulsifiers and stabilisers are also used to bind fat into sausages and pies, for example, which may result in people eating more fat than they realise. They also help to disguise the use of blood, bones, offal and skin in place of meat.

Polyphosphates are emulsifiers and have been used mainly to add water to poultry and cooked meat products. They permit from 4–120 per cent extra water to be incorporated, depending on the product. On the basis of taste tests, some manufacturers have argued strongly that consumers prefer the more succulent texture which the addition of water creates. Other consumers, however, criticise the volume of water released when cooking a chicken, object to paying the same price per pound for added water as for chicken flesh, and have pressed for products containing added water to be labelled accordingly.

The extensive use of polyphosphates in cooked meats is also questionable. One retailer told us that in their food tests the products which have polyphosphates are always preferred, but they were willing to acknowledge that this may be due to people's conditioning to expect a particular texture. Retailers told us that meat products on delicatessen counters may have a quite different composition and additive content from those which are pre-packed, although the minimum meat content is regulated. Inadequate labels do not allow comparisons to be made.

The real issues are whether additives improve, or merely alter, the texture, whether adding water debases the quality, and whether you can tell how much has been added. In most EEC countries, the use of polyphosphates is prohibited, although it remains widespread in the UK. In response to consumer pressure, some retailers have stopped selling polyphosphated poultry: others have never found it necessary to add them.

Variety and choice

As has been seen in other chapters, people want variety and a choice of food products, and are willing to pay for convenience. The use of gelling agents, for example, allows fruit purées to be made into a range of consistencies from jams to jellies and fruit pie fillings. Table margarines are made to resemble butter but their fat content is high, commonly over 80 per cent. People's demand for lower-calorie, low-fat spreads, resembling butter and margarine but with additional characteristics such as spreadability, low saturated fat content and acceptable taste, has been met by the use of additives in general and emulsifiers and stabilisers in particular.

Conversely, some people question whether they really need such a range of products, and suggest that the use of emulsifiers allows additional and unnecessary quantities of fat and sugar to be incorporated in food, thereby contributing to our over-consumption of these ingredients. In some instances, thickeners can mask the use of inferior quality ingredients, or, together with added colour and flavour, suggest that more fruit, for example, has been used than is the case. At the same time, some retailers have a significant demand for an economy range of products, and the use of this group of additives enables cheaper products to be made available.

Products which would not otherwise exist

Some products are wholly artificial and could not exist without complex emulsification and stabilisation systems. Notable in this category are the instant desserts and whips, coffee creamers, gravy granules, margarines and low-fat spreads. Arguably, none of these are essential for consumers, yet they add choice and most are supplied purely for convenience. All have established their place in the food market.

Emulsifiers and stabilisers are commonly found in the comparatively new chilled salads which are now widely available in supermarkets. They stop the salad dressings separating, and influence the texture.

Manufacturers' needs

Technical need

Manufacturers claim that there is a widespread need for emulsifiers, stabilisers, thickeners and gelling agents, and that because this group of additives performs so many different functions, all those currently permitted are required for at least one purpose.

Emulsifiers are used to disperse evenly two or more substances which would otherwise not mix. They ensure uniform quality and stability during the shelf-life of the product. Gum arabic (acacia, E414) used in confectionery, and tragacanth gum (E413) used in salad dressings and processed cheese, are the most widely used as they are stable in a wide range of products with different levels of acidity. Without emulsifiers, fat would float on the surface of ice-cream and margarine would separate.

The choice of emulsifier depends on the technological function in the end product. Cocoa butter used in chocolate manufacture may crystallise at high temperature. Emulsifiers such as sorbitan tristearate (492) are extensively used to prevent this in confectionery, and other additives perform a similar role in the manufacture of margarine. They also improve the creaming and baking performance of shortenings for pastry.

Emulsifiers can be used to simplify and control mixing processes. They may be used in different quantities in chocolate, depending on whether the chocolate is being moulded into bars, or for coating or decorating confectionery, for example.

Emulsifiers are also used in bread dough. They may be incorporated in general bread improvers, and enable loaves to retain the gases formed by the yeast. This results in a bigger loaf with a lighter texture and softer crumb, or more air, depending on which way you look at it.

By interacting with starch, emulsifiers prevent bread going stale so quickly and pasta products or instant mashed potato getting sticky. Polyoxyethylene compounds (430–436) have been used for this purpose since the 1940s, and they are also used as a substitute for some of the fat.

In egg-processing, excessive foam produced by whipping may cause manufacturing problems. Emulsifiers act as anti-foaming agents to reduce this tendency. On the other hand, extract of quillaia, which produces a froth when shaken with water, has been used for about 100 years to give a good head on some soft drinks.

Because they are so versatile, many of these additives are used for more than one function. In some ice-creams, for example, one emulsifier and stabiliser is combined with another to give an antioxidant effect.

The technical functions performed by stabilisers also vary. They prevent the separation of oils and fats which have been mixed into emulsions, but they can also be used to bind water in meats such as ham and sausage, thereby increasing their weight. Stabilisers may be used to prevent the oil separating out of peanut butter, for example. Phosphates may be added as stabilisers to concentrated milk. Many food products, such as instant desserts, cake mixes and whipped cream, are primarily emulsions which are whipped and aerated to form a foam. Such products are normally stabilised (to stop them collapsing) by using an agent such as propylene glycol alginate (E405) or lactylated mono-glycerides (E472b). These not only produce a stable foam, but improve stiffness and increase the volume of the end product.

Several of these additives thicken as well as stabilise foods. This is the case with agar (E406), carrageenan (E407) and sodium alginate (E401), all of which originate from seaweeds and act as gelling agents and stabilisers in desserts, ice-cream, processed cheeses and salad dressings. The gums thicken and stabilise soup mixes, sauces, salad dressings and some soft drinks. While natural starches can be used in cold mixes, modified starches increase the range of applications, by adapting the thickness, dispersibility and ease of gelatinisation, particularly in hot substances.

Quantities needed in individual foods

Even if a technical need for these additives can be established, the question of whether so much of each additive is needed in each food, remains. The quantity used varies from product to product. Since some products could not be made without complex emulsification systems, they are clearly essential if we want those products to remain available. For others, the need to use texture modifiers is determined by the method of manufacture.

Whether there is a technical need for texture modifiers to be used in the quantities currently permitted requires further study. In 1979, the food industry stated that this group was the most important class of additive for which there was a need for comprehensive data on use, but there is still no published information on how much we are all eating or whether daily intake exceeds internationally recommended acceptable levels.

The FAC in the past concluded that good manufacturing practice would be sufficient to ensure that only the minimum amounts necessary would be used, but whether this remains true might be worth questioning.

Alternative methods

As with other additives, manufacturers frequently have an option of using natural ingredients or additives. The main natural emulsifiers are lecithin in egg yolk, and casein, the protein present in milk which is used in meat and sausage products, cream soups and sauces, pastry and dairy products. Egg albumen is also an important aerating agent in baked goods as it can be whipped to form a stiff and stable foam.

Natural emulsifiers are effective under certain processing conditions. One retailer told us that in the process of reviewing their products, one variety of lemon curd was found to contain four emulsifiers. The company discovered that by increasing the quantity of egg, and hence the natural lecithin, the other emulsifiers could be removed. The revised product was considered to be of a higher quality, better texture, and was cheaper to make and buy than previously.

Do we need so many?

The number of texture modifiers has increased in recent years. Emulsifier manufacturers claim that the new additives can better meet the needs of the modern food processing industry. They speak of better fat distribution, enhanced palatability, creamier effects, and better control over the flow of liquids during processing. But then, they have an interest in creating the technical need for their products, and there has been no independent technical assessment of need in recent years.

The Food and Drink Federation consulted its members on the issue and was informed that there was still a technical need for all the emulsifiers currently permitted. Yet not all countries permit the use of emulsifiers, and some are considerably more restrictive about their application than we are in the UK. For example, Portugal and Israel prohibit the use of emulsifiers in bread; in France, emulsifiers and thickeners may not be added to processed fruit; and in many EEC countries they may not be used in frozen vegetables. It is not sufficient to suggest that because an additive is not used in another country, it is not necessary. It does, however, suggest that their general use in food is worthy of review.

Economic need

The economic need for emulsifiers and thickening agents in many products is a matter of judgement, and their use in recent years has expanded substantially as they have become cheaper than alternative ingredients: by 1984 the annual demand by UK manufacturers for emulsifiers, thickeners and stabilisers was estimated to be 68,000 tonnes, with a market value of £62 million per year. For example, in the UK, the use of butter or margarine in ice-cream was decreasing to the point at which it was becoming a rarity (although it has had something of a revival in the last few years). Butter and cream are generally found only in true Cornish ice-cream and some continental varieties. The product known as 'ice-cream' in the UK is a mixture of milk solids, sugar, flavouring, colour, emulsifier and stabiliser. The emulsifier improves the whipping quality of the mix and produces a smooth texture. It is not necessary, however, in ice-creams made the traditional way using butter and cream. The latter are, inevitably, more expensive.

The lemon curd example above shows that emulsification systems need not be the cheapest means of producing a good-quality product, although there are many examples of emulsifiers being used to reduce the cost of raw materials, or increase volume, without increasing the ingredients. For this reason manufacturers have been accused of using some of these additives to mislead consumers, and to retain their profits at the expense of quality. Such arguments remain largely theoretical, because only the manufacturers have access to the relevant information on comparative costs.

Trading standards officers point to a reduction in the quality of some canned fruit products, confectionery and bakery goods as a result of the increasing use of emulsifiers and thickening agents. But when the products would not exist without the additives, there is no standard against which to measure quality. Furthermore, their use in products like ice-cream and chocolate enables a cheaper alternative to be made available which increases choice, even though some people will also consider it to be a lower-quality alternative to the more traditional and more expensive versions.

Are they safe?

Unlike most other groups of additives, there has been little criticism of the safety of the texture modifiers as a whole. This stems in part from their widespread availability in natural food products, and the contribution which they have made for centuries to most people's diet without apparent ill-effects. However, evidence has come to light of potential safety hazards with a few of these additives, while others such as gums, starches, and celluloses, which are from plant sources, have not all been tested to modern standards.

One emulsifier, **carrageenan (E407)**, has been the cause of some concern – indeed, one retailer informed us that they would not use it in their products. Following the publication of articles in the *Lancet*, which suggested that it could cause ulcers in the colon and could be most harmful when taken in a drink, a thorough reappraisal of the toxicological status of carrageenan was undertaken by JECFA in 1984, and a distinction drawn between 'native' carrageenan obtained from seaweed, and a degraded form which is not apparently used in food. It is the degraded carrageenan which has given rise to toxic effects in animal experiments. Since this form of carrageenan is apparently not used in food, this evidence is of limited relevance for humans. Laxative effects have also been seen in animal experiments using 15 per cent carrageenan, but in food the emulsifying and gelling properties can be achieved at concentrations as low as 0.01 per cent, so the laxative properties are not thought to be significant for people. JECFA thought that no limits on the amount of carrageenan which could safely be consumed in the diet were necessary; the COT gave carrageenan an 'A' rating in 1970, and has not considered it in recent years.

In 1984 the EEC decided to ban the **polyoxyethylene stearates (430 and 431)** following an unfavourable report by the SCF. Polyoxyethylene (8) stearate (430) had been shown to cause cancer in animals; additive 431, being related to it, might do so too. There was also a suggestion that they may play a part in the formation of kidney stones. No ill-effects showed up in human experiments, and it is not thought to present a risk of cancer. However, to ensure that people were not put at risk, the EEC decided to prohibit its use. Yet despite Britain's obligations to implement the EEC's decisions, polyoxyethylene stearates remain on the UK permitted list pending revision. Lack of comprehensive data on the use of additives makes it impossible to say whether they are still used in food made in the UK.

The SCF was satisfied in 1983 with the albeit short and unrepresentative evidence for the **polysorbates,** based on polysorbate (60) alone. JECFA considered some of the polysorbates in 1982, and noted that they appeared to bring on diarrhoea in rats and hamsters. Kidney and liver changes were also noted in short-term studies in rats and monkeys. (These findings were not confirmed by long-term studies, but these were rather old.) Polysorbates have not been considered in recent years in the UK.

The most extensively used thickeners, the **modified starches,** are not subject to control in the UK and so may not have been comprehensively assessed for safety. Some are produced from physically modified starches and others from chemically treated starches. The method of treatment affects the safety assessment. In recommending that this group should be regulated by means of a permitted list, the FAC considered the toxicological evidence available and thought that there could be hazards to consumers from some of those in use at the time. Nine were recommended as safe, and a further three satisfactory pending further information and evidence of need. Despite this, limits were recommended on the use of certain modified starches in baby foods, pending EEC controls, although these recommendations have not been implemented.

The situation is not satisfactory: since the name of the starch does not have to be declared, consumers are unable to identify whether those currently in use are only those which were recommended, or whether others continue to be used in food while doubts about safety remain. All should be adequately tested and subjected to thorough toxicological assessment, like other permitted additives.

Action points

The example of the lemon curd earlier in the chapter shows that texture modifiers are not always necessary, but since they have received little attention from consumers, retailers or manufacturers, we were given little information about their real value and necessity when carrying out research for this book. Insofar as they may bind additional fat or water into products, they may reduce the quality of some foods, and you may in particular wish to avoid meats containing polyphosphates for that reason.

Polyoxyethylene stearates (430 and 431) *Since these have been banned in the EEC since 1984 it is unlikely that they are still used in food in the UK.*

8
Stopping the rot

To supply enough food to meet the needs of the mainly urban population of Western Europe during different seasons, much of the food produced must be preserved. There are many ways of doing this including canning, bottling, freezing, chilling, pasteurising and drying. The addition of preservatives increases the options available to food-processing companies.

Using additives to preserve food is not a recent phenomenon. The ancient Greeks burnt sulphur over wine in the cask, thus producing sulphur dioxide – this is still used in wine-making. Salting, smoking, adding alcohol, sugar and vinegar also have a long history of use. The most common methods relied, for example, on sugar to make jam, and on salt to cure meat. Both remain important preserving agents, but as they affect the taste and texture of the food, they are not always the most appropriate preservatives.

Preservatives kill or inhibit the growth of micro-organisms, such as bacteria, fungi, mould and yeasts, which would otherwise cause food to decay and possibly create health hazards. Antioxidants slow down or stop the process by which oils and fats become rancid on exposure to oxygen in the air. They also prevent fruit and vegetables going brown when cut and exposed to oxygen, and prevent added colours and flavours changing or fading in use. Foods containing fat may become rancid more quickly by the action of very small traces of copper or iron. Sequestrants may be used to prevent such trace metals taking part in the change; the most common is citric acid (E330), which is also an antioxidant.

Both preservatives and antioxidants are used to extend the

shelf-life of many processed foods such as bread, cooked meats, cheese, jams, pickles, soft drinks and desserts – anything which remains on the shelves in food shops for some time. Most food prepared with fats or oils, from meat pies to salad creams, is likely to contain an antioxidant. The maximum quantities and the foods in which particular preservatives and antioxidants may be used are laid down by law.

Consumers' needs

Food poisoning

Preservatives protect consumers against the presence of potentially dangerous micro-organisms, which either are naturally present or develop as food deteriorates.

If food is kept for too long without preservatives or antioxidants, changes take place. Fats, cheese and cream turn rancid, which affects the smell and taste of the food, and bacteria multiply in meat and fish, causing it to smell and possibly create a risk of food poisoning. Bacteria act on proteins and sugar in milk, making it go sour and curdle, while yeast from the peel of fruit in juice ferments natural sugars into alcohol and carbon dioxide.

Most of these changes are not dangerous, but they make food unappetising, and result in waste. However, some changes *are* dangerous. For instance, the notorious salmonella bacterium, if it is allowed to grow, can cause severe food poisoning, but it needs to be present in large numbers if it is to do so. It should be killed by heat treatment, provided the food is properly stored and thoroughly cooked. Botulism, the most serious form of food poisoning, can be lethal.

Other bacteria, however, are heat-resistant: while pasteurising kills the bacteria capable of causing tuberculosis, for example, it does not kill all micro-organisms. Milk, fruit juices and some cooked meats (for use in delicatessens) are pasteurised, not sterilised (at a much higher temperature). Preservatives may not be strictly necessary, but will give added protection for meats, particularly during the summer months, and will enable fruit juices to last longer after opening. They need to be kept chilled and used quickly if preservatives are not used. Preservatives are not permitted in milk. Bacillus and clostridia are heat-resistant, and survive the temperatures used, for example, in processing cheese. Since cheese offers a favourable climate for the growth of spores which could spoil it, nisin (234) is used as a preservative in some varieties.

Freezing and chilling prevent the growth of micro-organisms, but do not destroy them, so frozen meats may need preservatives so that they won't deteriorate while thawing, or when they are to be warmed up but not recooked.

About 20,000 cases of food poisoning are reported in the UK every year and this number has been rising, but this may have nothing to do with whether preservatives are used or not. Some countries which permit fewer preservatives experience less of a problem: higher standards of hygiene both in people's homes and in large catering establishments have been suggested as possible reasons for this.

Year-round supplies

People have become used to a wide variety of products with different keeping qualities. Without preservatives, or food which has been preserved in some way, they would have to shop more often, and would not be able to get hold of as many products out of season. Wastage at home and in the shops would increase, and this would add to the total cost of food. Food manufacturers stress that without the use of preservatives and antioxidants they would be unable to supply sufficient food to meet demand. However, we now have highly developed distribution systems which enable a variety of products with short shelf-lives, such as milk and meat, to be sold; and some people suggest that other methods of preservation could reduce the need for preservatives.

In the case of bread, for instance, people are getting used to shopping for it more often than before, or stopping it deteriorating by keeping it in the fridge or freezer. When the preservative propionic acid (E280) was removed from bread the shelf-life was reduced from 4–5 days to 1–2 days. The public was largely unaware that this was going to happen, and many people complained that mould started to grow on bread after only a couple of days. Adding vinegar (which contains acetic acid, similar to propionic acid) has extended the shelf-life a little.

Choice and variety

The use of preservatives adds to the variety of products available by extending their keeping qualities. Hence, fruit drinks, squashes and mixer drinks need preservatives if they are to be kept in a cupboard and continually opened and closed over a period of months. This may also be necessary in some sauces or pickles, depending on the amount of natural preservatives such as sugar or vinegar in the product. Without preservatives, fruit drinks and high-juice squashes must be kept in the fridge and used within a limited time. The same is true of low-sugar jams and fruit spreads without added sugar or preservative. Even with antioxidants, low-fat spreads and margarines have a limited life, and need to be kept chilled.

Some products would not exist as we know them without preservatives. Since the nature of bacon and ham depends on the curing process, which also preserves it, without nitrites there would be no bacon. Nitrites also give bacon and ham their characteristic flavour and colour, which currently cannot be achieved using other methods of preservation.

Manufacturers' needs

Technical need

In our researches, we found that companies were questioning their approach towards the use of antioxidants and preservatives. Many changes had occurred: for example, margarine manufacturers now often use citric acid and vitamin E rather than BHA/BHT, and fruit juice may be pasteurised instead of having chemicals added. Companies with a policy of reducing the additives in their foods are finding that they have an option not only of which additives to use, but of whether to use an alternative method of processing and packaging.

In general, the products from which manufacturers have been removing preservatives are those such as yoghurts and crisps where the preservative and the antioxidant respectively are not required to perform a function in the final product. In both instances the additive was to protect an ingredient (the fruit in the yoghurt, the oil used to fry crisps), but improvements in the quality of the raw materials, and hygiene in the factories, have removed the technical need.

Extending the shelf-life of products

The use of antioxidants and preservatives is one of the main areas where consumers' need and manufacturers' need for additives overlap to a considerable extent. Consumers want their food to last long enough for them not to have to shop every day. Manufacturers need time for sufficient quantities to be distributed and sold. The shelf-life required by retailers differs according to the level of demand, and the characteristics of the product itself.

In general, small shops need a much longer life for their products than multiple retailers. Not only is their turnover much slower, but they do not have the same degree of control over the distribution chain. Major food retailers can oversee the distribution of their products from farm or factory through to the point of sale. The small grocer is not so well placed: few manufacturers deliver direct to small shops, so a shopkeeper who is dependent on a çash and carry warehouse for supplies will have to collect more frequently to ensure high food quality. The shopkeeper may not know how the product was transported from the factory to the warehouse, or whether there was a delay in putting it into cold store, and he probably does not have the means to refrigerate supplies during transportation to the shop. So these products must contain added preservatives, or have been preserved in a way that will give them a sufficient shelf-life to avoid wastage and guarantee consumer safety.

Beer manufacturers pointed out to us that export varieties require a longer shelf-life than those produced for the home market. Sulphur dioxide (E220), benzoic acid (E210) and the hydroxybenzoates (E214–19) are preservatives permitted in beer, while sulphur dioxide and sorbic acid (E200) may be used in wine to protect the ingredients before, during or after processing. Preservatives are permitted in cheeses, too, since imported varieties such as Edam and those with added ingredients and flavours are claimed to need them for a sufficient shelf-life.

Some flavours, colours and enzymes need to be preserved before being used in foods in order to remain stable over the shelf-life of the product. Antioxidants also help foods to retain their natural colour while on display.

In considering antioxidants, the FAC has said that manufacturers are not justified in using them just to increase an already adequate shelf-life of a product. This provokes a whole range of questions about how shelf-life can and should be defined, and whether the use of the additive is essential, gives additional protection, or is merely commercially advantageous.

Backing up other forms of preservation

Dehydration is a standard method of preserving food but during the process some fruit and vegetables go brown. The only known method for preventing this is to use sulphites (E220–6), which may be added to the water in which the food is blanched before drying, or sprayed on. They may also be used to improve the appearance of dehydrated meat such as pork and chicken, to control browning on peeled potatoes and frozen chips, or to fumigate fresh grapes.

Sulphites also preserve the red colour in meat products such as sausages, speed up the process by which dough for bread, pastry and biscuits is made, and can be added to the juice of canned fruit.

Replacing natural preservatives and antioxidants lost in processing

Natural fats and oils contain antioxidants. These remain if the oil is mechanically pressed or extracted from the seed using solvents. Heat used in the extraction process, or when the oils are used for cooking, as in crisps, destroys the natural antioxidant, so it must be replaced with an appropriate additive.

Overcoming hygiene problems

Hygiene in factories is not always as high as modern standards would demand. Bacterial spores are commonly found in food-processing plants, and preservatives may need to be added to food to prevent contamination during processing. 'Rope', which causes bread to smell and become stringy in texture, results from the presence of bacteria. In the past, fruit intended for yoghurts was treated with additives so that it did not become contaminated beforehand, but one company told us that they had been able to remove the preservative by limiting the time between delivery and use, heat-treating the fruit, and reducing the risk of contamination from packaging left lying around the factory.

Airborne yeasts and moulds can spoil food, causing prepared salads, for example, to ferment and develop a sharp taste. Bacon may also suffer from micro-organisms which are present in the factory.

Fluctuations in temperature in the factory may also affect the quality of some products. They can, for example, alter the thickness and stability of mayonnaise, while sugar may become lumpy.

The FAC has said that preservatives are not an alternative to satisfactory hygiene and processing standards, but whether they are used in this way has not been subject to scrutiny. It cannot be justified as a 'technical need' but still seems to be accepted as one.

Economic need

The question of economic need hardly seems to have been addressed by regulatory bodies. Because preservatives and anti-oxidants are used in small amounts, their market value is much lower than that of other additives. For example, it was estimated that in 1984 about 1,600 tonnes of preservative were manufactured in the UK, with a value of only £1.5 million (out of a market value for all additives of £231 million). One hundred tonnes of antioxidants had a value of only £500,000.

Adding preservatives may be cheaper than alternative processing methods, or, even if more expensive, may be preferred by manufacturers for technical reasons. The financial benefit of extending the shelf-life of products is likely to be greater than the cost of adding individual preservatives.

If retailers over-estimate the demand for a product with a limited shelf-life, food spoilage and waste can cause them substantial losses. A wholesaler told us that when preservatives were first removed from bread, independent retailers reduced their purchases substantially so that they would sell out daily as none would have wished to be left with large supplies. Major retailers build such losses into their turnover, but small traders find them more difficult to cover.

The need for preservatives to be added to exports, and to imported varieties for sale in the UK, underlines the role which they can play in maintaining the competitiveness of industry. Some years ago, when considering a request for antioxidants to be allowed in the base used for chewing gum, the industry successfully argued that the natural antioxidants were destroyed during the purification process. Since an antioxidant was allowed in Australia, New Zealand and Canada, the UK industry was at a disadvantage. The addition of BHT, it was claimed, doubled the shelf-life and led to a better quality product. The use was agreed and is now permitted (but see also below under 'Additives of particular concern').

Safety considerations

All the preservatives and antioxidants used in the UK have been assessed by the COT and the EEC's SCF, and have also been reviewed internationally. Considerable concern has been expressed about the safety of sulphites, nitrites, BHA, BHT and the gallates, so these additives have been subject to continual review and appraisal. The bodies responsible have declared that all are acceptable for use in food at the levels currently permitted, but that as new evidence becomes available they will continue to review their safety. At present only the antioxidants with vitamin properties have category 'A' status (see Chapter 2), and while this was also given to several of the preservatives, these have not been the subject of a comprehensive review in the UK since 1972.

For these additives more than any others, the safety of the individual substances has to be weighed against the comparative risks from the development of toxins during processing and storage. For example, it might not make sense to remove a preservative which presented a risk to a small number of people, if it meant putting the wider population at risk from food poisoning.

All the retailers and manufacturers we spoke to said that they would not be willing to remove preservatives from any product if this would reduce safety levels. They are conscious of their liability if someone's health suffers as a result of eating one of their products. All believe that the use of preservatives is essential if consumers are not to be put at risk. At the same time, while accepting the technical need for nitrites to cure bacon and ham, several said they were concerned at possible health risks arising from the preservative itself, and would use an alternative if a satisfactory one could be found. (See also under 'Food poisoning' earlier in the chapter.)

Additives of particular concern
Nitrates and nitrites (E249–52)
These preservatives are particularly effective against the bacteria which cause botulism and salmonella poisoning, which can otherwise be eliminated only at very high temperatures. Nitrates and nitrites may be converted by bacteria in the body into nitrosamines, many of which are known to cause cancer in animals and which can also lead to foetal abnormalities. The significance of this for humans has not yet been established, but there has been sufficient concern for the FAC to have stated more than once that their use should be phased out. Fifteen years after it was first suggested that they be banned, they remain in use, although the levels used have been continually reduced in recent years. No alternatives have been found which are as effective against *Clostridium botulinum* and which allow pork to be cured to form bacon and ham.

Interestingly, a report published by MAFF in 1987 indicated that the intake of nitrites and nitrates from raw vegetables and water was likely to be higher than that from processed food.

Sulphur dioxide and the sulphites (E220–26)

These are extensively used as food additives because they are comparatively cheap and can be used as anti-microbial agents, enzyme inhibitors, antioxidants and agents to control browning. They are generally considered to be not particularly toxic but have come under public scrutiny following the death of several asthmatics in the USA, who had adverse reactions to sulphur dioxide which had been used to 'refresh' salads in a catering establishment. Very few cases of adverse reactions have been reported, even among asthmatics, but those who are at risk may suffer asthma attacks, dermatitis, gastric irritation or lowered blood pressure after consuming even very low levels of sulphite.

Sulphiting fresh food is not allowed in the UK but there are many products on sale in which its use does not have to be declared, the most notable being beer and wine. But the presence of preservatives also need not be declared when sulphited fruit is used in jam, or when sulphited fruit or nuts are used as ingredients for cereals, cottage cheese or other products. Sulphites pose no risk to the majority of the population.

The benzoates (E210–19)

These can induce adverse reactions (including nettlerash and asthma) in some people, particularly asthmatics or those who are sensitive to aspirin. Given their widespread use, it is possible for people to consume in one day more than the amounts known to induce adverse reactions.

BHA/BHT (E320/E321)

When food is stored, it gradually loses vitamins A and E. Antioxidants prevent that. BHA and BHT are specifically permitted for this purpose in foods containing vitamin A, but there are other ways of reducing the loss of vitamins, such as by using light-proof materials and gas packaging.

These antioxidants have been the subject of controversy since the 1960s, when the FAC first commented that the margin of safety for BHT was less than that for the other permitted antioxidants, and that its use should be discontinued unless there were overriding technological advantages.

More recent concerns focus on the possibility that BHT could cause cancer at high doses, as suggested by the results of some animal studies; this is not borne out by others. BHA is known to cause cancer in rats but the possible effects on man are not known. Recent evidence also suggests that BHA can affect chromosomes in cells. The COT is awaiting further information on both these additives.

BHA and BHT can cause adverse reactions such as contact dermatitis in people who are allergic to aspirin. The extent of the problem and whether children are particularly at risk is not known, but the numbers are thought to be very low even among allergy sufferers.

The gallates (E310–12)

Although these additives are similar in structure to BHA and BHT, they do not appear to produce the same effects in animal experiments, and the COT does not consider them to be carcinogenic. However, there has been insufficient research to ensure that they do not cause mutagenic effects, so the COT has requested further tests.

Over-consumption?

We don't know exactly how many preservatives and antioxidants are eaten in an average daily diet. For some of the preservatives, such as the benzoates, the acceptable daily intakes were set in the early 1970s and have not been re-evaluated since.

There is concern that children who consume a lot of soft drinks and packaged foods may exceed the acceptable quantity of sulphur dioxide.

In tests for *Which?* magazine, Consumers' Association found that amounts of sulphite in some wines are close to the maximum permitted levels. *Which?* estimated that by drinking a quarter of a litre of white wine and one third of a litre of red wine, it is possible to exceed the ADI.

Safer alternatives

Over the years, food manufacturers have persistently argued that, despite concerns over safety, there are no satisfactory alternatives to the nitrites, nitrates, BHA and BHT, for example. These claims have not been subjected to independent assessment in recent years.

One supplier of nisin has been arguing that since this has not been found to have toxic or allergic effects, it could be used to extend the shelf-life of dairy desserts, milk products, beer and spirits – such uses are currently prohibited in the UK. Nisin is the only preservative permitted in the UK which is not on the EEC's fully authorised list. This is because it is an antibiotic, and scientific opinion is agreed that antibiotics used in human medicine should not be permitted in food. It is permitted only in cheese, clotted cream and canned foods, and in foods which incorporate one of these as an ingredient; it is effective against the bacteria that cause botulism and can virtually eliminate spoilage at a relatively low level of heat. There are no limits on how much of it may be used. But if the population were to become resistant to certain antibiotics that are necessary for health, because of their increasing use in food, this could have other long-term effects on safety.

In the United States research has been under way to try to find alternatives to nitrites as antioxidants in cooked pork. Some success has been achieved in using combinations of ascorbates with polyphosphates. In taste tests people did not detect any difference between nitrite-cured pork and pork treated in the new way.

Time to tighten up?

In 1972, the FAC laid down conditions which should be taken into account when considering the need for preservatives. Noting that most foods are subject to attack by yeasts, moulds and bacteria at ordinary temperatures, and that food manufacturing and distribution should be organised so that the food reaches the consumer in a wholesome, nutritious and palatable state, it commented that:

- good hygiene and modern packaging are necessary to prevent spoilage and reduce wastage
- both in production and storage, at all levels of distribution, preservation should as far as possible be by physical means such as sterilisation, pasteurisation and refrigeration
- the use of specific chemical preservatives should be allowed only when the desired effect cannot be obtained by manufacturing practices which are both economically and technologically satisfactory, and where the advantages clearly outweigh any possible disadvantages.

Little has been said in official reports about how the need for antioxidants should be defined, what would be a 'reasonable' shelf-life for products with and without them, and whether there are particular products in which their use is essential. In 1963, however, the FAC commented that 'an antioxidant should be allowed . . . only when there is evidence of real need, and not merely some minor commercial advantage, and when its use is likely to benefit the consumer without presenting a foreseeable hazard to health'.

Despite this, and continuing concerns over safety, the FAC has agreed to requests for additional uses for antioxidants. For example, in 1974 it was agreed that either BHA or BHT or a mixture could be used in potato powder, flakes and granules. Manufacturers argued successfully that this led to a better quality product, substantially longer shelf-life without deterioration of the flavour, and that gas packing was not a completely satisfactory alternative.

Although preservatives and antioxidants are subject to greater control than any other additives, there has been no comprehensive review of their need and use in recent years. Yet during this time the number of permitted preservatives has been increased, as has the range of foods in which they may be used. Additional requests for them to be permitted in soup concentrates, fillings and toppings for cakes and biscuits, and fruit pieces in syrup, have been approved.

Because preservatives are biologically active compounds, the features which make them valuable as preservatives may also act upon humans. Thus, their safety is not guaranteed, and their use should be limited to the products in which they are essential. To assess the validity of using additives to prevent food spoilage, it is necessary to look at the range of other methods of preservation available – these have become increasingly sophisticated in recent years. The availability of refrigerated and frozen foods has expanded greatly, and conventional canning now competes with food sterilised in trays. Packaging improvements, such as the use of opaque packets to exclude light, or gases to keep out oxygen, as well as aseptic packaging, have all extended the shelf-life of products.

The FAC also has to consider whether the shelf-life considered by manufacturers and retailers to be necessary for a product, is in fact appropriate. The required shelf-life will often be the factor which determines the level of preservative which is necessary. Whereas some manufacturers produce and sell vegetable oils without added antioxidants, a wholesaler who supplies small shops told us that they needed a shelf-life of nine months for vegetable oils, and their products required an antioxidant. Modern distribution systems and date marking have enabled some retailers to sell products with a short shelf-life.

Different countries interpret need for preservatives differently based on demand for different products and purposes. In France for example, since wine consumption is high, people may exceed the acceptable daily intake of sulphur dioxide just from wine. It may not, therefore, be used as a preservative in food, but alternatives are permitted. The USA and Japan do not permit the gallates, but use other antioxidants which are not allowed in the UK. BHA has been banned in Japan, and BHT is not permitted in Australia, South Africa or Switzerland. While different countries follow different policies, most permit a range of antioxidants and preservatives to be used.

There is some evidence that the FAC has not been as stringent in determining the case of need as might be desirable. Would preservatives be needed if factory conditions were improved?

Are preservatives and antioxidants needed to the extent to which they are used in frozen products, and could the levels of use be further limited? Should food served in catering establishments be allowed to contain higher levels of preservative than food for retail sale?

If preservatives are genuinely needed to protect health, consumers will not question their use, but until the FAC updates its views on the use of preservatives and antioxidants, looks at the alternatives and informs people of the findings, consumers will continue to voice concern.

Action points

If you wish to consume products containing fewer preservatives, you will need to shop regularly and must follow strictly the advice given about the time within which the food should be consumed. You will not be able to see the bacteria which cause food poisoning and there may be no noticeable smell or evidence of deterioration. The message should be: 'If in doubt – throw it out.' The majority of preservatives are used for a purpose, and manufacturers and retailers consider the risk to health from food poisoning to be far greater than that from additives.

If you wish to avoid particular additives which may be toxic or are associated with adverse reactions, you might want to look out for:

Sodium nitrate and the nitrites *In most cooked meats, sausages and bacon, in milk used for some cheeses, and in pizzas.*

Sulphur dioxide and the sulphates *In a wide variety of foods, including sausages, canned meats, fruit products, soft drinks, wine, beer and instant potato products.*

The benzoates *In soft drinks, jams, beer, fruit products and juices, desserts, salad cream, fish products, sauces and pie fillings.*

BHA/BHT *In vegetable oils, chewing gum, stock cubes, cheese spreads, biscuits, pies, pastry and packet convenience foods.*

The gallates *In vegetable oils, margarine, instant potato products, snack foods and chewing gum.*

9
Miscellaneous additives

In addition to the additives described in earlier chapters, there are more than 150 which are less well known. They are regulated by a permitted list of miscellaneous additives (see the back of the book for the full list). There are also some categories for which regulations have not yet been drawn up — additives in these groups may be used in food provided they do not pose a threat to people's health. Regulations for some of the unregulated groups are planned as part of the EEC's programme to make food legislation consistent in all Community countries.

Additives covered by regulations

Acids
Apart from their use as flavours, acids are used, for example, to free carbon dioxide gas in raising agents, and to adjust acidity which helps jam to set. They may also be used to dissolve food colours, or to preserve food. The most commonly used acids are citric, malic and lactic. Citric acid (E330) occurs naturally in citrus fruit, but is prepared commercially by the fermentation of molasses. It is mainly used in soft drinks and confectionery as a flavour, but also regulates the acidity of products and enhances the effect of other additives. It is used in wine, cider, tinned fruit, sauces, ice-cream, dried packet mixes, jam, cheese, crisps, bakery products, frozen fish, chips, potato products and marmalade. Other acids available to manufacturers include acetic (E260 — used widely in pickles, mayonnaise, salads, bread and fish products), and phosphoric (E338 — added to cola drinks for its sour taste).

Anti-caking agents

These prevent food particles sticking together: table salt, powdered milk and icing sugar, for instance, often contain an agent to stop them going lumpy. Examples include magnesium carbonate (504) for icing sugar, and calcium silicate (552), which also acts as a release agent (see below) in sweet manufacture.

Anti-foaming agents

These prevent liquids boiling over by breaking down foams and reducing scum. They also stop liquids frothing when they are being bottled. Glyceride oils (which are also used as emulsifiers) and silicones are the most common. Dimethylpolysiloxane (900) is added to some beers to reduce the amount of head on them.

Bases (alkalis)

These additives, which include the hydroxides (524–528), decrease the acidity of foods such as sweets, and also help dissolve acidic substances such as some colourings. They may react with acids to produce gassy raising agents and aerate products.

Bleaching and improving agents

These bleach and artificially speed up the maturing of flour, to make bread dough easier to process. They also improve the rising behaviour and consistency of different wheats, particularly the soft British wheat. They include potassium bromate (924), benzoyl peroxide, chlorine (925) and azodicarbonamide (927).

Buffers

Examples are calcium gluconate (578) and the orthophosphates (E339–E340), which hold the acid-alkali balance constant when more of an acid or alkaline substance is added.

Bulking agents

Manufacturers use these to add bulk without calories or nutrients, so you get the impression of eating more than you are. They are therefore used particularly in slimming foods but may also extend ingredients or replace more expensive ones. Alphacellulose (E460) and polydextrose are the most common.

UNDERSTANDING ADDITIVES

Excipients
These are used as dry carriers for other powdered additives, to make the mixture more manageable. Sorbitan monostearate (491) acts as a carrier for the flavours, preservatives and colours used in cream fillings.

Firming and crisping agents
These are sometimes added to tinned fruit and vegetables, pickled cabbage and some frozen vegetables in order to make the processed food retain its firmness. They include calcium chloride (509), calcium hydroxide (526) and calcium malate (352).

Glazing agents
These are mainly waxes and oils which produce a shine on food; they may also have a preservative effect. The gloss on dried fruit (raisins and apricots) is given by added mineral oils such as liquid paraffin (905). Dextrin is used to produce a polished look on sweets.

Humectants
These prevent food drying out and becoming hard and unpalatable. Sorbitol (E420) is used in pastries and packaged cakes, and glycerol (E422) in cake-icing and sweets. Sugar may achieve a similar effect.

Liquid freezants
Liquefied gases such as liquid nitrogen extract heat from foods and freeze them by direct contact. They are used particularly on items such as strawberries which need to be frozen quickly. Dichlorodifluoromethane is also used for this purpose.

Propellants
These gases or highly volatile liquids are used to expel foods from aerosol containers. As examples, nitrous oxide is added to cream in aerosol cans and dinitrogen monoxide is used for foaming whipped cream.

Release agents
These substances are used to prevent food sticking to food-processing equipment, packaging, moulds, tins, conveyor belts or machinery. They are usually greases or powders and are spread or dusted on to surfaces or coated on to food to make it non-stick. Talc and silicates (551–553b) are used to dust the moulds for making sweets, and polyglycerol esters of polycondensed fatty acids of vegetable oils for greasing baking tins.

Sequestrants
These attach themselves to trace metals, thereby slowing down the process of food deterioration (see the section on antioxidants in Chapter 7).

Solvents
Carrier solvents can dissolve food or a component of food; carry other additives; and help process raw materials. They help to disperse nutrients, emulsifiers, colours or flavours through food. Propane-1,2-diol alginate (E405) is used as a carrier for flavours. Ethyl alcohol or ethanol is used in many colouring and flavouring agents. Some also function as extraction solvents, but these are not separately regulated in the UK. They extract ingredients such as flavours or fats from raw materials or food products. Dichloromethane extracts caffeine from coffee or tea, and oils and fats from fish.

Substances which are not regulated
The FAC has been reviewing all the unregulated additives in order to complete the UK regulations and specify on permitted lists all the additives for use in food.

Among the additives which the Committee has not yet reviewed are processing aids such as finings and other clarifying agents, encapsulating agents, diluents, whipping aids, tableting aids, artificial smoke solutions, and crystallisation inhibitors. These are not currently subject to any control other than the general requirements of the Food Act 1984, that food shall not be injurious to health (although some additives which perform these particular functions are already permitted for other purposes).

Enzymes are biological catalysts which make possible certain technical processes; there is some difference of opinion as to whether they should be categorised as additives. Rennet turns milk into junket or cheese; proteolytic enzymes are used as meat tenderisers and prevent cloudiness in soft drinks; carbohydrate-splitting enzymes are used to clear fruit syrups while pectin-splitting enzymes facilitate the pressing and filtration of juice from fruit; others again help with fermentation in the brewing and baking industries.

Modified starches were mentioned in Chapter 7 since they act as thickeners. They have not, however, been regulated as additives, although the EEC intends that they should be and has allocated E numbers to some. The FAC has also recommended that they should be regulated by means of a permitted list, and did not consider that all types of modification were safe.

Limits on use

Although all the miscellaneous additives on the permitted list may be used in food in the UK, some have had restrictions placed on either the foods in which they may be used or the quantities. For example, metatartaric acid (353) may be used in only small quantities in wine. Bleaching agents are permissible in limited quantities only in bread and flour. Bulking aids may not be added to foods specially prepared for babies or young children. Some release agents are also restricted to certain foods, and are not permitted as additives by other EEC countries. Aluminium potassium sulphate, a firming agent, may be used only in glacé cherries.

Mineral hydrocarbons and solvents are regulated separately from the other miscellaneous additives. There is a short permitted list of solvents, but the controls on mineral hydrocarbons are not typical since they do not specify a permitted list, and ban the use of hydrocarbons except in certain foods, such as dried fruit (prunes, currants, sultanas and raisins), citrus fruits, sweets and any foods into which they have been carried over in ingredients.

Consumers' needs

It is probably impossible to assess consumers' needs for such a diverse group of substances, some of which are very versatile and can be used in a number of ways in different products, while others have very specialised uses. The one thing they have in common is that they increase the range of products available.

For example, the use of carbon dioxide in fizzy drinks enables consumers to benefit from a wider choice of products, as does the use of raising agents in baking. But some products which were traditionally made using these additives are now facing competition from alternatives without: for example, beer without added carbon dioxide is now available, although the lack of labelling on alcoholic drinks could make it difficult to find.

Medical opinion differs about the role of salt in contributing to high blood pressure. Both the National Advisory Committee on Nutrition Education (NACNE) and the Committee on the Medical Aspects of Food (COMA) recommend that we do not increase our salt intake, and that cutting it down might be beneficial; it certainly will not be harmful. Manufacturers have responded to this by marketing a range of low-sodium alternatives to salt, and by replacing sodium chloride (the ingredient we know as salt) with other salty-tasting substances in food. As in the case of sweeteners, it is debatable whether consumers 'need' these substances, since they may be better advised merely to reduce their liking for salty flavours. However, there is a demand for such products, which are usually made up of potassium chloride (508) alone or a mixture of salt and potassium chloride.

Health concerns, combined with changing food technology, have led to a demand for decaffeinated coffee and tea. There are several ways of removing caffeine from coffee beans including high-pressure washing, and using solvents. However, labels are at present not required to divulge the process by which the caffeine has been removed, so consumers are not able to make a real choice between products treated in different ways.

Some people who wish to diet find the use of bulking aids in food helps them to satisfy their demand for food, while reducing calorie intake. Bulking aids are used primarily in diet foods, and can be taken before or during a meal to fill the stomach and reduce the appetite. Bulking aids are used at significantly higher levels than most additives to achieve their effect. Because they are not necessary as part of a normal diet, they are not permitted in foods for children and young infants.

Some additives have made it possible to present traditional foods in new forms. Hence the use of expellants now allows cream to be produced in aerosol cans as a convenient way of creating a professional effect. Whipping agents are also added. Acids are used to produce sour cream, which might otherwise be achieved by adding lemon juice to cream at home.

Manufacturers' needs

Technical need

Very little information is available about the real technical need for this vast range of additives. Companies interviewed by us predictably stated that they would not use an additive which was not technically necessary, since they follow good manufacturing practice, and would not in any case wish to spend money unnecessarily. Earlier chapters have shown, however, that need has from time to time been exaggerated, or may be governed by traditional practice rather than current requirements given changes over time. The nature of the UK regulatory system ensures, almost inevitably, that the emphasis is on getting additional additives approved, rather than making sure that the best ones are fulfilling the required function.

For some groups the technical need can be shown clearly. For example, enzymes enable manufacturers to control the required change in a product, as we have seen. Although many enzymes are used in the preparation and processing of food, they are not present in the final product. The FAC says that residues are frequently very small indeed. However, the FAC accepts that there is a need for enzymes for use in food, and in 1982 recommended that 42 should be controlled by a permitted list; 29 of these had not been comprehensively assessed and had category 'B' status (see Chapter 2). It also proposed that enzymes should meet prescribed specifications, but so far no government has implemented the recommendations.

There is a clear technical need for enzymes to be used to make products such as cheese, which depend on them for their basic consistency, or as processing aids to obtain pectin from fruit, for example. But the desirability of enzymes being used to speed up natural processes may be more questionable. Many manufacturers use papain to tenderise meat for use in ready meals, beefburgers, steaklets and the like. In effect, the enzyme acts rather like the enzymes in our stomachs and starts to digest the meat so that it seems less chewy. This enables manufacturers to make lower quality meat seem less tough than it would be naturally, and may help some consumers by keeping prices down. The debate centres on whether this misleads people about the quality of what they are buying.

The FAC is considering whether enzymes should be permitted to speed up the process by which cheese has traditionally been matured. Manufacturers argue that using the enzymes will significantly cut their costs, and thus increase competitiveness against foreign suppliers. These arguments may seem attractive but could result in many traditional cheese-makers going out of business, with a loss of choice and reduction in quality in a traditional product which contributes significantly to the diet. On the other hand, a cheaper 'enzyme-matured cheese' might provide a useful source of protein for people on low incomes.

Over the years manufacturers defined a technical need for a substantial number of processing aids which perform no function in the final product. Processing aids can be of incidental benefit to consumers only if they help to reduce production costs without leaving residues which serve no purpose in the final product.

Widely used processing aids include the clarifying or fining agents in soft and alcoholic drinks; these remove particles which would otherwise make liquid cloudy. Casein extracted from milk, dried blood and china clay is used for this purpose. It forms a sediment with the particles it removes and the liquid can be syphoned off – thus any residue is very small.

Non-stick agents, and free-flow agents which speed the flow of substances though machinery, are also widely used. There may be scope for reducing this: one retailer informed us that he had asked a manufacturer to remove a free-flow agent from one of their products as they did not consider it necessary.

There is a technical need for some substances to complement others in the manufacturing process. Hence, sequestrants are used with antioxidants, and synergists will increase the effect of particular antioxidants. The presence of an acid may enhance a sour flavour, or contribute to a preservative effect by creating an acid environment in which bacteria find it more difficult to grow. Often in processed foods more than one acid is necessary to prolong shelf-life.

Where the quality of the raw materials varies, as in the case of beer- or wine-making, additives may be needed to offset the natural variations in the product and ensure that quality is maintained. Hence it is permitted to add tartaric acid (naturally present in grapes) if the grapes from hot climates are lacking in acidity, or to add chalk (calcium carbonate) to musts which are too acid as a result of a lack of sun. The chalk combines with the excess natural acid and both are then removed.

What are the limits?
In considering the need for some of the new classes of additives, the FAC has indicated certain limits: miscellaneous additives should not, for example, be used to mislead people about the quality and content of the food they are eating. It did not, for example, endorse a request for an enzyme which would remove the residues of penicillin from the milk of cows which had been treated for mastitis, since it considered that any milk containing antibiotics was contaminated. Using an additive to remove another unwanted substance from a product which was not of consumable quality was not accepted as a valid technical need. The Committee took the view that additives should not be used to cover up deterioration in a product, or to make a product appear to be of better quality than it is.

It also turned down a request for certain new additives which would be used to cloud soft drinks, since a number of permitted additives (such as stabilisers) and natural food substances currently used for this purpose, were considered to be doing a satisfactory job already.

Some people consider that among some of the groups of miscellaneous additives, too many are permitted for similar functions. As an example, the range of flour improvers, treatment agents and raising agents permitted in the UK allows for a wide range of bread, bakery products, cakes and biscuits. However, in order to produce a standard white loaf, these treatment agents need a range of other additives if they are to work. But they are not always necessary, as has been shown by the widespread removal of bleach from white flour, with no apparent decrease in quality.

Furthermore, is it necessary to permit as many as twelve additives to clarify wine, and another nine to reduce the loss of carbohydrate and control the breakdown of proteins when malting for beer?

Economic need

Whether they are needed or not, the use of additives does enable some manufacturers to cut down on their costs, and pass some of the savings on to customers. By using commercially prepared enzymes, for example, brewers can save on the quantity and quality of grain used; enzymes can be used to tenderise low quality cuts of meat; sequestrants and acids can be added to products to give them a longer shelf-life than they would otherwise have. Retailers told us that there is a definite demand for an economy range of products. The problem, though, is that people are not supplied with enough information with which to weigh up quality against cost in order to make an appropriate choice.

Economic factors result in unacceptable ways of using additives, such as to add weight without cost to products. The use of polyphosphates for this purpose was mentioned in Chapter 7. Glazing agents may also have this effect: although prawns, for instance, need to be protected during cold storage, so that the surface does not dry out, heavy ice glazes may mean that the consumer is paying for a product that is 40 per cent ice glaze and only 60 per cent prawn. Improved labelling is beginning to answer this problem.

Safety factors

All the additives on the miscellaneous permitted list have undergone some toxicological testing and been approved for use in the UK. However, 83 of them have not yet been fully evaluated by the SCF, and many have not been considered by the COT in recent years, and may therefore not have been subjected to the same degree of analysis as is required of new additives.

In 1985, for example, MAFF noted that the time limits set by the SCF for review of certain solvents had expired, and called upon industry to supply additional information on the solvents whose safety was still not assured. One such was 1,2-dichloro-ethane: the SCF was not prepared to recommend its temporary use because of conflicting results in animal studies which indicated potential cancer-inducing properties. Mutagenic responses had also been witnessed in bacteria, and there was evidence of interaction with certain food constituents which could be toxic under extreme conditions. Three other solvents – butyl acetate, ethyl acetate and hexane – were given only temporary approval by the COT pending further information on their toxicity.

Some of the bases, such as sodium carbonate (500), may cause gastric upsets and circulation problems if consumed in very large amounts. Ammonium chloride (510) and magnesium sulphate – Epsom salts (518) – should be avoided by people with imperfect liver or kidney functions, but this may also be true of other additives. Small babies and people suffering from kidney and heart complaints should avoid sodium sulphate (514) and sodium aluminium phosphate (541). But people are unlikely to find them on labels as they will be classified as processing aids, or carried over in ingredients. Evidence of such adverse reactions is limited but this is not to say that they do not occur. The problem of identifying when these agents are used in food, and the fact that many are added in very small amounts would make detection difficult.

If citric acid is used in very large quantities, it may occasionally cause erosion of the teeth and irritation in or around the mouth. It may contribute to dental decay through the formation of plaque, and along with tripotassium citrate (E332) is known to provoke mouth ulcers. Irritant effects are also found with tartaric acid (E334) which, if consumed in undiluted form, may cause gastro-enteritis, and has been used medically for its laxative properties.

Lactic acid was reviewed as long ago as 1973 by JECFA which expressed concern for babies who suffered acidosis and weight-loss in tests with milk containing DL-lactic acid. A number of babies could not tolerate it, and they suffered diarrhoea and weight-loss. The effects were reversible when the acid was removed, but it would be preferable if it were not used in foods likely to be consumed by very young children. JECFA noted that humans have consumed fruits, sour milk and other products containing this acid for centuries, but that does not mean that it is without any effects.

Some of the flour treatment agents have given rise to unsatis-factory results in animal experiments. Potassium bromate (924) produced kidney cancer in rats and is mutagenic in a range of cells. In humans it can cause nausea, vomiting, diarrhoea and severe abdominal pain. Azodicarbonamide has also been shown to be mutagenic, although JECFA concluded that it is not car-cinogenic. Although JECFA has set maximum levels for the use of flour treatment agents, which should result in very low intakes. It also says that the residues left after processing are so low that they are not detectable. However, their safety has not been unequivocally assured and in 1988 potassium bromate was given only temporary clearance.

Some concern has also been expressed regarding the phos-phates. While they may limit dental decay, the main worry relates to the effects of altering the balance of calcium, magnesium and phosphate in the diet. Numerous animal studies have shown that excessive dietary phosphorus causes an increase in phosphorus in the blood and loss of calcium, which can affect the bones. There is uncertainty about the optimum ratio of these nutrients and whether the calcium:phosphorus ratio has any significance for humans.

The future

New additives are being developed all the time, and requests are made for more and more to be placed on permitted lists for particular purposes. It is high time that miscellaneous additives were subjected to a comprehensive review. The criteria for continuing to permit an additive should not merely be because manufacturers consider it necessary, or because it is known that some still use the substance.

The EEC has suggested that one criterion for assessing need should be that the proposed function cannot be achieved in any other way, and that the additive does not present a hazard. That leads on to a whole range of questions about whether the function itself is necessary and desirable, as well as the possibility of using alternative processing methods which may be preferable for consumers.

Different countries view the use of additives in different ways and few permit as many for use generally in food as the UK. In some countries the use of processing aids is not regulated with additives, and where countries have lists which separately regulate the various functions of additives, their miscellaneous lists appear much shorter. However, since processing aids do leave residues in food, it is appropriate that their safety should be controlled with additives and their use declared. It is not just a question of whether they are safe, or could affect our health. It is more a question of restricting to an absolute minimum the use in food of those substances which have no nutritional value. This, after all, is a fundamental requirement of the Food Act 1984 and places a duty on Ministers to ensure that it is met. It appears at present that it may not be.

Action points

There are a wide variety of miscellaneous additives, many of which are regulated and approved for use in the UK. Not all have been considered in this chapter. Most are processing aids, some of which may leave small amounts of residue in the foods you eat. If used as processing aids, they will not necessarily be declared on the labels, so there is little that the consumer can do.

10
Choosing to avoid additives – a shopper's guide

It is almost impossible to follow a diet which is completely free from all additives. Indeed, it is probably not desirable, since some have nutritional properties and may impart essential vitamins or minerals.

For most of the population, there does not appear to be a risk to health from consuming additives in general. There are, however, a number of specific additives over which there are questions of safety, or which cause adverse reactions in some people, and others which this book has shown are necessary only to produce choice and variety of food products. You may wish to avoid these or indeed others according to your own personal views.

Additives you may wish to avoid

Colours (Chapter 4)
Amaranth (E123)
Annatto (E160b)
Brilliant blue FCF (133)
Caramel (E150)
Chocolate brown HT (155)
Indigo carmine (E132)
Ponceau 4R (E124)
Quinoline yellow (E104)
Sunset yellow FCF (E110)
Yellow 2G (107)
Black PN (E151)
Brown FK (154)
Carmoisine (E122)
Erythrosine (E127)

Patent blue V (E131)
Pigment rubine (E180)
Red 2G (128)
Tartrazine (E102)

Flavour enhancers (Chapter 5)
Monosodium glutamate (621)
Guanosine (627)
Inosine (631)
Sodium 5'-ribonucleotide (635)

Sweeteners (Chapter 6)
Aspartame
Saccharin

UNDERSTANDING ADDITIVES

Emulsifiers (Chapter 7)
Polyphosphates (E450)
Polyoxyethylene stearates
 (430 and 431)

Preservatives (Chapter 8)
Sodium nitrate and the nitrites
 (E249–E252)
Sulphur dioxide and the sulphates
 (E220–E227)

The benzoates (E210–E219)
The sorbates (E200–E203)

Antioxidants (Chapter 8)
BHA (E320)
BHT (E321)
The gallates (E310–E312)

How can you identify products without them?

We approached fifteen of the leading retail food chains, including frozen food stores, and five of the wholesale cash and carry companies which supply small grocers, asking all of them the following questions:

- what is your policy on the use of additives?
- how is the policy put into action?
- what information can you make available to consumers who wish to know more about your policy?
- has the composition of your own-label foods been reviewed in order to reduce the use of additives?
- which of your own-label products are free of additives?

All companies told us that the situation was changing from day to day, and that any information could be out of date almost as soon as it was issued. Some companies who were reviewing their policies were unable to give us the detailed information we sought.

It is almost impossible to compare one supermarket with another, because their policies are quite diverse, ranging from those which have taken virtually no steps to reduce additive use, to those which have been reviewing the content of all their own-brands to see whether the additives in use are really needed, and are removing those which are either unnecessary or which have given public concern.

In view of public concern about certain artificial colours, most companies have reviewed their use, particularly in products eaten by children. Squashes, yoghurts and snack products have been widely reformulated and now if they are coloured at all they commonly contain natural colours and flavours.

If you wish to avoid certain additives, your main task will be to look at the labels because there is no other way to identify specific additives in individual products. Even that will not tell you the full story (as Chapter 3 shows). For many people, however, doing a weekly or monthly shop for food is a tedious and lengthy task. It is quite unrealistic to check the content of all the foods you buy. If, however, you do most of your shopping at one supermarket, you may find it helpful to know what policy the company follows, and to look at the lists of products which are free from particular types of additives before you go shopping.

Not all companies can supply information on additive-free products. Some small retailers do not have the information at all. Some keep lists just of foods free from artificial colours, others of those free from preservatives or monosodium glutamate, and some maintain lists of products free from what the company defines as 'contentious' additives.

If you do manage to get hold of lists of products which do not contain particular categories of additive, you may still be misled. As we have said, the lists soon become out of date, and the fact that a company has no 'additive-free' products in a particular category may just mean that the company does not stock any products in that category among its own-label foods, and not that such products are unavailable in the store.

From the information we received, it appears that you will be able to find a wide variety of tinned fruits, vegetables and baked beans which are free from additives. Additive-free cereals and some biscuits are available, although nutrients and additives may have been added to flour in the product, or carried over on dried fruit, and these are unlikely to be listed. Most dried rice, pulses, beans and pasta are additive-free. Among dairy products, a wide variety of cheeses and many yoghurts do not contain additives, but you would need to check to be sure.

Very few meat products (other than fresh meat) contain no additives at all. Exceptions can be found in chilled and frozen meals, and in some varieties of beefburger; some canned fish and fish pâtés are also prepared without additives. Increasingly, fresh quiches and flans are additive-free. In most supermarkets, there appears to be only a limited range of own-label cakes without additives, but it depends on the suppliers and the desired shelf-life. Among soft drinks, if you want an additive-free variety, you are likely to have to rely on fruit juice, rather than a fruit drink, and it is difficult to find squash without preservatives, added colour or flavour.

Among the products which it is virtually impossible to obtain without additives are those such as instant desserts, coffee creamers and some salad dressings, which cannot exist without the accompanying additives. If you want additive-free ready-made desserts, you will need on the whole to choose frozen or fresh varieties. Although some specialised varieties of sausage can be found without additives, most fresh and frozen sausage contains preservative, and may also contain colour, antioxidants and phosphates. Products such as pizzas, which contain some cooked meats, will also usually have additives in the ingredients, but there is a choice. Dried soups may contain additives, as do most of the tinned varieties. Many pickles, sauces and dressings also have additives. Jams in the cheaper price ranges need additives such as gelatine to ensure that they set and are of a consistent quality, although an increasing number of fruit spreads and high quality jams are made without additives. Many wines, beers, spirits and ciders contain additives, but as they are not currently labelled, their contents are not known, and brewers are willing to inform consumers only in exceptional circumstances.

Company policies

Most of the companies which we approached supplied us with detailed information on their policies.

Boots do not sell the full range of foodstuffs, but have a range of diet, diabetic and vegetarian foods, soft drinks and an increasing range of 'healthy foods/snacks'. Their policy is to keep the use of additives to a minimum, and not to use any additives of which the safety has been questioned, or which are considered to be contentious, except where they are essential for preservation. The company continually questions the use of all additives and evaluates new information. It is removing all the artificial colours and flavours, caramel, BHA/BHT and MSG from its range, and when introducing new products aims to keep additive content as low as possible.

Bejam have produced *Food Facts*, a booklet which gives nutritional information on over 300 of its products. This includes a classification of those products which contain 'no artificial colour' and those which contain no 'artificial additives'. The company claims that more than 95 per cent of its products are free from artificial colour, alternative colours having been substituted. People with specific dietary requirements are, however, advised to consult ingredients lists.

Co-operative Wholesale Society is untypical of most of those we spoke to because it manufactures as well as retails many of its products. The society's policy is to reduce use of additives to a minimum where it is appropriate and safe to do so. Where new products are developed, priority is given to additive-free varieties, and cosmetic additives perceived as artificial are being replaced.

Gateway informed us: 'We have been asking our suppliers to remove additives from any product that it is possible to remove them from . . . but this will not be done if the change is detrimental to taste or distribution of the product.'

Iceland, who specialise in frozen foods, stress that freezing is a natural method of food preparation, and that many of their products have always been additive-free. Since 1986, the company has actively removed artificial additives from its own-label products, concentrating on removing artificial colours, flavours, preservatives and MSG, replacing the last with herbs and spices. All raw materials are traced back to source, and carry-over must be declared. They have published a booklet, *Nutrition and Additive Guide*, which lists all own-label products and gives their additive content. It is regularly updated. The foods are classified by product group, and divided into frozen, grocery and chilled products.

Littlewoods have produced lists for circulation within the company of additives which they consider to be contentious. Some of these are banned from their own-label foods. A more extensive list of additives is under review, and the safety and need for all of these are being considered. The company has informed its suppliers of this policy, and is implementing it throughout the range. The priorities are to remove colours, antioxidants, flavour enhancers, preservatives and artificial flavours. So far 450 lines have been reviewed, and action has included the removal of most artificial colours, some antioxidants and preservatives, and MSG from some meat products.

Marks and Spencer supplied us with a combined list of products which were free from artificial colours, flavours and preservatives, but they would not meet us to discuss the policy. Because M&S have a policy of selling fresh foods, often with a very short shelf-life, they are able to offer varieties of biscuits, bread, cakes, soups, frozen and chilled desserts that are free from additives in those groups. Such products don't appear to be available in other stores. M&S are the only company which listed a wide range of chilled meat products, as well as frozen and fresh pizzas, flans and pies, as free from colours, flavours and preservatives.

William Morrison, while committed in principle to removing additives which are unacceptable to their customers, in practice appear to lag behind some of their competitors. Initially they did not want to respond to what were seen as the views of a vociferous minority, but as manufacturers started to offer alternatives, and children's safety was questioned, the company began to implement changes where they did not affect the quality of products. Now that the company recognises the public disquiet, it is scrutinising the need for additives in new products. New leaflets in support of a healthy eating campaign have been produced, but they do not cover additives, which are not seen to be a major marketing issue.

Nurdin and Peacock are wholesale suppliers for independent grocers and other shops. They began to respond to consumer trends several years ago, and have tried to remove azo dyes from their products. However, as suppliers of small shops and caterers, they do not have the power of the large retailers to influence suppliers, and have mainly responded to the trends which manufacturers have set. Nevertheless, the company did ban the use of tartrazine in own-brand products, but considers that industry should be able to use additives which, once pronounced safe, contribute to the development of commercially attractive products.

Presto is a trading division of Argyll foods, whose stated policy is to avoid the use of additives both in the branded goods it purchases and its own-label goods. They are in the process of implementing this policy and plan to remove any additives which are 'found to contribute nothing and where their removal does not make the product unacceptable to the customer'. Products free from additives are classified into 26 categories, but with the exception of products such as cheese, pasta, tea, coffee, cereals and frozen foods, there are as yet few varieties which are additive-free.

Safeway was one of the first of the supermarket chains to respond to public concern about additives, by publishing a list of more than 50 additives which they wanted to remove, if possible and practical, from their own-label products. These included all the additives which were considered to be associated with adverse reactions. Their priorities were to remove artificial colours (especially azo dyes), preservatives (benzoic acid and sulphur dioxide), BHA/BHT and MSG, and replace them if necessary with alternatives. They did not find it possible to remove completely all those additives on their 'contentious' list, and the most rapid progress was made in removing colours. Nevertheless, several hundred products have been reformulated. A review of the content of products is continuing. Safeway produce a list of products 'free from contentious and artificial additives' and require manufacturers to declare on the packaging any additives contained in ingredients used in the final product. Two booklets are also available – *Additives: Why do we need them?* and *Additives: What are they?*

UNDERSTANDING ADDITIVES

Sainsbury began to review the formulation of all their own-label products early in 1985, questioning whether all additives were needed. The aim was to remove those which were unnecessary, and priority was given to products consumed by children, such as squashes, ice-cream, yoghurts and fish fingers. So far more than 800 products have been reviewed, with modifications made particularly in the use of colours, some preservatives and MSG – lists are available of items free from these additives and of those products free of all additives. These lists are regularly updated. It is increasingly possible to find new products without additives. The company gives details of the purposes for which the additives are used, and reasons why people may wish to avoid them. Those food groups in which the additives are not used at all are given, as well as the specific foods which are additive-free.

Spar aim to remove all unnecessary additives, and where practicable to remove or replace additives which are 'emotive' to the consumer. Among those cited as having been the subject of consumers' interest are tartrazine and BHT. Spar wrote to all suppliers to establish the practicality of removing these substances, and obtained varied responses. They have been able to make limited changes with existing suppliers and where manufacturers' own formulations have changed. Changes are not made if they will affect the quality, keeping properties or sales potential of products. The company is also very aware of the constraints which affect independent grocers, who need longer shelf-lives than supermarkets.

Tesco have been reviewing the composition of and use of additives in all their products since October 1985. Those additives about which there has been most concern, particularly regarding adverse reactions, have been identified. So far about 500 products have had their specifications changed, and the company claims that more than 50 per cent of its products are now free from unnecessary additives. Azo dyes, BHA/BHT and some preservatives have come in for particular attention. Technologists are required to justify the use of additives in particular products, and it is anticipated that a further 1,000 will be reviewed over the next twelve months. When new products are launched, particular care is taken to ensure that no unnecessary additives are used, and about 400 products are now additive-free. Unlike some companies, when Tesco describe products as additive-free, they mean that no additives have been used in the product, either as an ingredient or a processing aid. Lists of products which are free from additives are available on request.

Waitrose aim to sell foods which are 'wholesome, safe and as natural as possible'. With this in mind, all products have been reviewed, to see whether all additives are needed. In many cases it has been possible to remove all additives; in other cases natural ones have been used to replace artificial ones. Special attention has been given to certain artificial additives for which a list of those known to be of concern to customers was drawn up. The company does not introduce additive-free alternatives if the product is of a lower quality as a result. It declares additives carried over from ingredients, and has produced a guide called *Additive Free Foods and Nutrition Information*.

Appendix

The laws and procedures for assessing safety and regulating the use of food additives

The United Kingdom

All additives in use in food in the UK must conform with the requirements of the **Food Act 1984.** This prohibits the addition of any substance which renders food 'injurious to health', and means that manufacturers face criminal penalties if they use ingredients in food which prove not to be safe. This very general clause is all that governs the majority of additives in use in the UK, including flavourings, enzymes, modified starches and some processing aids. In practice, however, since many of these substances are used in fairly small quantities and are not easily identifiable in food, and since it is exceptional for people to suffer ill-effects from the amount in a single food (unless they have a history of adverse reactions), an individual food manufacturer is most unlikely to be taken to court.

More helpful for ensuring public safety are the precise regulations covering specific groups of additives permitted for certain functions – **permitted lists.** Twenty-four categories of additive are regulated in this way. Some of these regulations also state the maximum amount of the substance which may be used, and/or the conditions of use, and the foods in which the additives may be included. This is the case for antioxidants, mineral hydrocarbons, preservatives and a few individually named additives. **Compositional regulations,** those which control the way certain foods are made up, also specify which additives may be used. For example, there are specific restrictions on the additives that can be used in jam, fruit squashes, cheese, bread and flour.

Two committees advise the Government on food additive regulations: **The Food Advisory Committee (FAC)** was set up by the Government to advise Ministers on the composition, labelling and advertising of food, and the additives, contaminants and other substances which are or may be present in food, or in its preparation. It considers requests by industry for new additives to be permitted. First, the FAC must be persuaded that the additive in question performs a function that existing permitted additives do not perform, or improves on an existing additive, or that its introduction could benefit consumers in some way. If the FAC decides that one of these criteria is met – in other words, that there is a case of need for the additive – the **Committee on Toxicity of Chemicals in Food, Consumer Products and the Environment (COT)** is asked to review the additive's safety and report to the FAC. If the COT's report on safety is positive, the FAC will recommend to the Government that the additive be permitted. The majority of additives are permitted for use in any foods, but some will be permitted for only certain purposes in certain amounts, and some will be permitted for only a period of time pending further evidence on a safety question.

The FAC is also responsible for any periodic reviews of groups of additives that are requested by Ministers, and for recommending any changes that are needed to the Government. The FAC reports incorporate the findings of the COT and sometimes of the **Ministry of Agriculture's Food Surveillance Group,** which looks at patterns of food consumption to see which food additives are used in and how much of specific additives the average person will be consuming. FAC reports are published for public comment, but the reports and comments are no more than recommendations to the Government. There have been few comprehensive reviews – the most recent one (on colours) took ten years to produce, so much of the information on patterns of consumption is now out of date.

The FAC's 15 members are appointed by the Ministers of Health and Agriculture who have a joint responsibility for the safety of food. The members act in an individual capacity, but they are intended to be broadly representative of industry, consumer, scientific and medical opinion. There are four representatives from industry, one from the retail trade, two enforcement officers, five from medical and academic backgrounds and three to cover consumers' interests.

The COT is appointed by the Minister of Health from members of the medical profession, academics and professional toxicologists who either work for food manufacturers or act as consultants for them.

The COT takes into account information on the chemical properties and method of manufacture of the additive. These are considered alongside the results of feeding experiments on animals, tests of the effects of the substance on cells, and any information arising from human studies or experience. In reality the research results are rarely clear-cut (see Chapter 2). Toxicological data are notoriously difficult to interpret, and the relevance of animal studies for man is a constant subject for debate. Thus, the COT has to make judgements both on limited available evidence and the balance of probabilities.

European Community Controls

Since the UK is a member of the EEC, it is involved in and influenced by the Community procedure for approving food additives. As part of its programme to establish an open market in which foodstuffs move freely between Community countries, the European Commission intends to standardise all Member States' controls on additives in order to ensure the safety and health of consumers and remove barriers to trade. These can arise, for example, when an additive permitted in one country is considered unsafe by another, or when the foods in which certain additives may be used differ from country to country.

The main groups of additives – colours, preservatives, antioxidants, emulsifiers, stabilisers, thickeners and gelling agents – are now subject to Community rules, but the majority of additive groups are not yet regulated at EEC level.

In drawing up proposals for regulations, the European Commission consults a range of bodies. Safety is considered by the **Scientific Committee for Food** (**SCF**), which operates in a broadly similar way to the UK's COT. On the basis of toxicological data, the SCF considers whether substances are acceptable for use, and if so, may establish acceptable daily intakes (ADIs) – maximum levels for the average intake of an additive by humans. The SCF has no remit to consider whether an additive is needed, however, and decisions on the foods in which the additives may be used are left to Member States, because food consumption patterns differ from one country to another. To ensure that the ADI is not generally exceeded, different countries have required different regulations.

The Commission may also ask for advice on proposed changes in regulations from the **Advisory Committee on Foodstuffs,** which includes representatives from industry, consumer organisations, trade associations, farmers and trade unions. The **European Parliament** and the **Economic and Social Committee** all have an opportunity to comment as well. The **Standing Committee on Foodstuffs** expresses the official views of the national governments on proposed legislation, while the SCF (see above) gives the opinion of toxicologists. But the **Council of Ministers** (comprising Ministers from each Member State) is responsible for deciding which additive may be used. Additives which are approved for general use by the Council of Ministers in the EEC are also assessed by the COT before legislation permits their use in the UK.

Worldwide networks

Internationally, under the auspices of the United Nations Food and Agriculture Organisation (FAO), and the World Health Organisation (WHO), there is a committee which monitors and evaluates food additives. This is the FAO/WHO Joint Expert Committee on Food Additives (JECFA), which was set up to 'formulate the general principles governing the use of food additives, with special reference to their legal authorisation'. JECFA evaluates the safety of additives internationally, and recommends maximum acceptable daily intakes (ADIs) on the basis of toxicological information. JECFA's views reflect the balance of international opinion. It has evaluated more than 700 food additives, and has produced a database covering the status of all those which it has assessed. This is updated annually. It is a valuable source of information, of particular assistance to those countries which are not able to carry out toxicological testing for themselves.

Index of additives

This index covers additives on permitted lists only (so flavours, modified starches, enzymes and so on do not appear). We list additives by number within each category, such as colours or sweeteners, followed by an alphabetical list of those without a number (see Chapter 3). The charts will tell you what types of food and drink each additive is likely to be found in, and, in the case of Miscellaneous additives, what function the additive performs (see Chapter 9). Not all of these additives are mentioned individually in the book, but page references are given for those that do appear. Mention in the text does not necessarily mean that the additive may have been associated with a question of safety.

Number	Name	Typical food uses	Page
Colours			
E100	curcumin	flour confectionery, margarine, processed cheese, vanilla ice-cream	71, 78, 90, 92
E101	riboflavin	sauces, processed cheese	57
101a	riboflavin-5'-phosphate	jams	57
E102	tartrazine	soft drinks, smoked yellow fish, salad cream, marzipan, convenience foods	45, 47, 54, 69, 75, 77, 78, 79, 88, 89, 92, 95, 159, 165, 166
E104	quinoline yellow	smoked yellow fish, Scotch eggs	89, 95, 159
107	yellow 2G	—	87, 95, 159
E110	sunset yellow FCF	biscuits, lemon curd, orange squash, packet soups	77, 78, 89, 92, 95, 159

Number	Name	Typical food uses	Page
E120	cochineal	alcoholic drinks	
E122	carmoisine	jams and preserves, jellies, blancmanges	62, 77, 88, 95, 159
E123	amaranth	packet soups, fruit pie fillings, gravy granules, canned fruit, ice-cream, jam, yoghurt	49, 50, 77, 87, 92, 95, 159
E124	ponceau 4R	dessert mixes	77, 89, 95, 159
E127	erythrosine	glacé cherries, canned cherries, strawberries and rhubarb, biscuits, sweets, chocolates, instant desserts, salmon spread, canned pie fillings, garlic sausage, salami, Scotch eggs	26–7, 42–3, 88, 89, 93, 95, 159
128	red 2G	sausages, cooked meats, meat pies, frozen meals	80, 88, 93, 95, 159
E131	patent blue V	desserts, confectionery, Scotch eggs	89, 95, 159
E132	indigo carmine	biscuits, sweets	89, 91, 95, 159
133	brilliant blue FCF	canned vegetables	49, 89, 95, 159
E140	chlorophyll	fats and oils, green vegetables preserved in a liquid	
E141	copper complexes of chlorophyll and chloro-phyllins	jellies, lime and lemon squashes, green sweets	84
E142	green S	fruit pastilles, mint sauce and jelly, canned peas	
E150	caramel	beer, some other alcoholic drinks, cola drinks, biscuits, sauces, soups, chocolates, bread, gravy browning, pickled onions, preserves, meat products, packet cake mixes, liquorice, sweets	54, 69, 77, 82, 84, 85–6, 90, 92, 95, 159, 163
E151	black PN	blackcurrant cheesecake mix	77, 95, 159

Number	Name	Typical food uses	Page
E153	carbon black (vegetable carbon)	liquorice, jams, jellies	90–1
154	brown FK	kippers, smoked mackerel, some crisps, the skin of cooked chicken	83, 87 93, 95 15
155	brown HT (chocolate brown HT)	chocolate cake, imitation chocolate products, preserves, pickles, some soft drinks	87, 95 15
E160a	alpha-carotene; beta-carotene; gamma-carotene	margarine, soft drinks, vanilla ice-cream, red Leicester cheese	57, 58 71, 78 81–2, 9
E160b	annatto; bixin; norbixin	crisps, margarine, kippers, red Leicester cheese	45–6, 66 71, 77 81, 8 91, 9 95, 15
E160c	capsanthin; capsorubin	processed cheese	9
E160d	lycopene		
E160e	beta-apo-8'-carotenal		
E160f	ethyl ester of beta-apo-8'-carotenoic acid		
E161a	flavoxanthin		
E161b	lutein		
E161c	cryptoxanthin		
E161d	rubixanthin		
E161e	violaxanthin		
E161f	rhodoxanthin		
E161g	canthaxanthin	used as fish feed to enhance colour of flesh	
E162	beetroot red (betanin)	ice-cream, liquorice, jams	
E163	anthocyanins	yoghurt, glacé cherries	27, 7 8
E171	titanium dioxide	sweets, horseradish sauce	
E172	iron oxides; iron hydroxides	packet cake mixes	
E173	aluminium	⎫	
E174	silver	⎬ cake decorations	
E175	gold	⎭	
E180	pigment rubine (lithol rubine BK)	used to colour cheese rind	95, 1

Number	Name	Typical food uses	Page
	methyl violet	used for the surface marking of citrus fruit	
	paprika	canned vegetables	77, 78, 91
	saffron; crocin	smoked cod and haddock	77, 78, 91
	sandalwood; santalin		77, 91
	turmeric	soups, vanilla ice-cream	77, 78, 90

Preservatives

Number	Name	Typical food uses	Page
E200	sorbic acid	soft drinks, fruit yoghurts, processed cheese slices	135, 160
E201	sodium sorbate		
E202	potassium sorbate	} frozen pizzas, cakes, biscuits	135, 160
E203	calcium sorbate		
E210	benzoic acid		
E211	sodium benzoate		
E212	potassium benzoate		
E213	calcium benzoate		
E214	ethyl 4-hydroxybenzoate (ethyl para-hydroxy-benzoate)		
E215	ethyl 4-hydroxybenzoate, sodium salt (sodium ethyl para-hydroxybenzoate)	beer, jam, salad cream, soft drinks, fruit pulp, fruit-based pie fillings, marinated herring and mackerel	46, 47 54, 135, 140, 141, 145, 160, 165
E216	propyl 4-hydroxybenzoate (propyl para-hydroxy-benzoate)		
E217	propyl 4-hydroxybenzoate, sodium salt (sodium propyl para-hydroxybenzoate)		
E218	methyl 4-hydroxybenzoate (methyl para-hydroxy-benzoate)		
E219	methyl 4-hydroxybenzoate, sodium salt (sodium methyl para-hydroxybenzoate)		

Number	Name	Typical food uses	Page
E220	sulphur dioxide		
E221	sodium sulphite	dried fruit, dehydrated	28, 46,
E222	sodium hydrogen sulphite (sodium bisulphite)	vegetables, fruit juices and syrups, sausages, fruit-based	54, 60, 62, 70,
E223	sodium metabisulphite	dairy desserts, biscuits, cider,	75, 82,
E224	potassium metabisulphite	beer, wine; also used to prevent	135, 136,
E226	calcium sulphite	browning of raw peeled	140,
E227	calcium hydrogen sulphite (calcium bisulphite)	potatoes	141–2, 144, 145, 160, 165
E230	biphenyl (diphenyl)		
E231	2-hydroxybiphenyl (ortho-phenylphenol)	surface treatment of citrus	
E232	sodium biphenyl-2-yl oxide (sodium orthophenyl-phenate)	fruit and nuts	
E233	2-(thiazol-4-yl) benzimida-zole (thiabendazole)	surface treatment of bananas	
234	nisin	cheese, clotted cream, canned foods	133, 142
E239	hexamine (hexamethylene-tetramine)	marinated herring and mackerel	
E249	potassium nitrite	bacon, ham, cured meats,	26, 44,
E250	sodium nitrite	corned beef, some cheeses,	54, 56–7,
E251	sodium nitrate	pizzas	134,
E252	potassium nitrate		138–9, 142, 145, 160
E280	propionic acid		
E281	sodium propionate	bread, buns, cakes, biscuits,	133–4
E282	calcium propionate	Christmas pudding	
E283	potassium propionate		

Number	Name	Typical food uses	Page

Antioxidants

Number	Name	Typical food uses	Page
E300	L-ascorbic acid (vitamin C)	fruit drinks, fruit jams and	26, 27,
E301	sodium L-ascorbate	preserves, beer, wine, dried	69, 142
E302	calcium L-ascorbate	potatoes, Scotch eggs, pork	
E304	6-0-palmitoyl-L-ascorbic acid (ascorbyl palmitate)	pies, sausages, canned meat; also used to improve flour and bread dough	
E306	extracts of natural origin rich in tocopherols		
E307	synthetic alpha-tocopherol	vegetable oils, cereal-based baby foods, sausages, dessert toppings	
E308	synthetic gamma-tocopherol		
E309	synthetic delta-tocopherol		
E310	propyl gallate	vegetable oils, chewing gum,	56, 141,
E311	octyl gallate	chicken soup, margarine,	145, 160
E312	dodecyl gallate	instant potato products	
E320	butylated hydroxyanisole (BHA)	beef stock cubes, cheese spread, margarine, savoury rice, fruit pies, sweets, biscuits, some potato snacks	29, 44, 46, 50, 56, 57, 134, 138, 140–1, 143, 145, 160, 163, 165, 166
E321	butylated hydroxytoluene (BHT)	chewing gum, salted peanuts, gravy granules, margarine, vegetable oils, pastry, instant mashed potato, dehydrated convenience foods	29, 44, 46, 50, 56, 57, 134, 138, 140–1, 143, 145, 160, 163, 165, 166
E322	lecithins	low-fat spreads; also used as an emulsifier in chocolate	
	diphenylamine	used to prevent discoloration	
	ethoxyquin	on apples and pears	

Number	Name	Typical food uses	Page

Emulsifiers and stabilisers

Number	Name	Typical food uses	Page
E400	alginic acid		
E401	sodium alginate		
E402	potassium alginate	ice-cream, soft cheese, cake mixes, salad dressings	124, 125, 149
E403	ammonium alginate		
E404	calcium alginate		
E405	propane-1,2-diol alginate (propylene glycol alginate)		
E406	agar	ice-cream, flavoured yoghurts, meringue	125
E407	carrageenan	quick-setting jellies, milk-shakes, instant mousses, biscuits, pastries, sausages, meat pies	69, 125, 128
E410	locust bean gum (carob gum)	salad cream, packet soups, meringue mixes, salad dressings, processed cheese, confectionery, sweet pickle, cole-slaw, soft cheese, sauces, pie fillings, water ices, canned vegetables, flavoured yoghurts, fruit gums, wine, beer	123
E412	guar gum		
E413	tragacanth		
E414	gum arabic (acacia)		
E415	xanthan gum		
416	karaya gum		
430	polyoxyethylene (8) stearate	bakery goods	128–9, 130, 160
431	polyoxyethylene (40) stearate	bread	124, 128-9, 130, 160
432	polyoxyethylene (20) sorbitan monolaurate (Polysorbate 20)	bakery products, confectionery creams, non-dairy coffee whiteners, sweets, ice-creams, frozen desserts	129
433	polyoxyethylene (20) sorbitan mono-oleate (Polysorbate 80)		
434	polyoxyethylene (20) sorbitan monopalmitate (Polysorbate 40)		
435	polyoxyethylene (20) sorbitan monostearate (Polysorbate 60)		
436	polyoxyethylene (20) sorbitan tristearate (Polysorbate 65)		

Number	Name	Typical food uses	Page
E440a	pectin	jams, preserves, puddings,	119, 120,
E440b	amidated pectin	flavoured yoghurts, ice-cream	153
442	ammonium phosphatides	cocoa and chocolate products	
E460	microcrystalline cellulose; alpha-cellulose (powdered cellulose)	high-fibre bread, grated and processed cheese	20, 56, 147
E461	methylcellulose	low-fat spreads	
E463	hydroxypropylcellulose		
E464	hydroxypropylmethyl-cellulose	edible ices, jellies	
E465	ethylmethylcellulose	gateaux	
E466	carboxymethylcellulose, sodium salt (CMC)	jellies, soft drinks, potato waffles, canned soups, tomato sauce, custard and dessert puddings, instant mashed potato	
E470	sodium, potassium and calcium salts of fatty acids	cake mixes	
E471	mono- and di-glycerides of fatty acids	frozen desserts	
E472a	acetic acid esters of mono- and di-glycerides of fatty acids	mousse mixes	
E472b	lactic acid esters of mono- and di-glycerides of fatty acids	dessert toppings	124–5
E472c	citric acid esters of mono- and di-glycerides of fatty acids	continental sausages	
E472e	mono-and diacetyltartaric acid esters of mono- and di-glycerides of fatty acids	bread, frozen pizza	
E473	sucrose esters of fatty acids		
E474	sucroglycerides	edible ices	
E475	polyglycerol esters of fatty acids	cakes and gateaux	
476	polyglycerol esters of polycondensed fatty acids of castor oil (polyglycerol polyricinoleate)	chocolate flavour coatings for cakes	

Number	Name	Typical food uses	Page
E477	propane-1,2-diol esters of fatty acids	instant desserts	
478	lactylated fatty acid esters of glycerol and propane-1,2-diol		
E481	sodium stearoyl-2-lactylate	bread, cakes, biscuits	
E482	calcium stearoyl-2-lactylate	gravy granules	
E483	stearyl tartrate		
491	sorbitan monostearate		
492	sorbitan tristearate		
493	sorbitan monolaurate	cake mixes	123, 148
494	sorbitan mono-oleate		
495	sorbitan monopalmitate		
	dioctyl sodium sulphosuccinate	used in sugar-refining to help crystallisation	
	extract of quillaia	used in soft drinks to generate foam	124
	oxidatively polymerised soya bean oil		
	polyglycerol esters of dimerised fatty acids of soya bean oil	used to grease bakery tins	149
	pectin extract	jam and preserves	

Sweeteners

Number	Name	Typical food uses	Page
E420	sorbitol; sorbitol syrup	sugar-free confectionery, jams for diabetics, soft-scoop ice-cream, sausages	110, 112, 114, 116, 148
E421	mannitol	sugar-free confectionery, chewing gum	110, 114, 115, 116
	acesulfame potassium (acesulfame K)	canned foods, soft drinks, table-top sweeteners	109, 111, 114
	aspartame	soft drinks, yoghurts, dessert and drink mixes, sweetening tablets	47, 109, 111, 115, 116, 117, 118, 159
	calcium saccharin	(same uses as saccharin below)	
	hydrogenated glucose syrup	sugar-free confectionery	109–10, 112, 116

Number	Name	Typical food uses	Page
	isomalt	sugar-free confectionery	110, 112, 114, 115, 116
	saccharin sodium saccharin	soft drinks, processed fruit, canned vegetables, bakery products, reduced sugar jams, cider, sweetening tablets, table-top sweeteners	48–50, 108–9, 111, 115, 118, 159
	thaumatin	table-top sweeteners, yoghurts	109, 111
	xylitol	sugar-free chewing gum	110, 112, 114, 116

Miscellaneous additives

E170	calcium carbonate (chalk)	base, firming agent, release agent, diluent; bakery products, sweets, wine, ice-cream	154
E260	acetic acid	acid/acidity regulators (buffers) used in pickles, salad cream and bread; they contribute to flavour and provide protection against mould growth	146
E261	potassium acetate		
E262	sodium hydrogen diacetate		
262	sodium acetate		
E263	calcium acetate	firming agent; also provides calcium which is useful in quick-set jelly mixes	
E270	lactic acid	acid/flavouring which protects against mould growth; salad dressing, soft margarine	
E290	carbon dioxide	carbonating agent/packaging gas and propellant; used in fizzy drinks	69, 151
296	DL-malic acid; L-malic acid	acid/flavouring; used in soft drinks, sweets, biscuits, dessert mixes, pie fillings	
297	fumaric acid		
E325	sodium lactate	buffer, humectant; used in jams, preserves, sweets, flour confectionery	
E326	potassium lactate	buffer; jams, preserves, jellies	

Number	Name	Typical food uses	Page
E327	calcium lactate	buffer, firming agent; canned fruit, pie fillings	
E330	citric acid		64, 97, 131, 134, 146, 157
E331	sodium dihydrogen citrate (monosodium citrate); disodium citrate; trisodium citrate	acid/flavourings, buffers, sequestrants, emulsifying salts, (calcium salts are firming agents); used in soft drinks, jams, preserves, sweets, UHT cream, processed cheese, canned fruit, dessert mixes, ice-cream	157
E332	potassium dihydrogen citrate (monopotassium citrate); tripotassium citrate		
E333	monocalcium citrate; dicalcium citrate; tricalcium citrate		
E334	L-(+)-tartaric acid	acid/flavourings, buffers, emulsifying salts, sequestrants; used in soft drinks, biscuit creams and fillings, sweets, jams, dessert mixes, processed cheese	154, 157
E335	monosodium L-(+)-tartrate; disodium L-(+)-tartrate		
E336	monopotassium L-(+)-tartrate (cream of tartar); dipotassium L-(+)-tartrate		
E337	potassium sodium L-(+)-tartrate		
E338	orthophosphoric acid (phosphoric acid)	acid/flavouring; soft drinks, cocoa	146
E339	sodium dihydrogen orthophosphate; disodium hydrogen orthophosphate; trisodium orthophosphate	buffers, sequestrants, emulsifying salts; used in dessert mixes, non-dairy creamers, processed cheese	
E340	potassium dihydrogen orthophosphate; di-potassium hydrogen orthophosphate; tri-potassium orthophosphate		
E341	calcium tetrahydrogen diorthophosphate; calcium hydrogen orthophosphate; tricalcium diortho-phosphate	firming agent, anti-caking agent, raising agent; cake mixes, baking powder, dessert mixes	

Number	Name	Typical food uses	Page
350	sodium malate; sodium hydrogen malate	buffers, humectants; jams, sweets, cakes, biscuits	
351	potassium malate		
352	calcium malate; calcium hydrogen malate	firming agent in processed fruit and vegetables	149
353	metatartaric acid	sequestrant used in wine	69, 150
355	adipic acid	buffer/flavouring; sweets, synthetic cream desserts	
363	succinic acid	buffer/flavouring; dry foods and beverage mixes	
370	1,4-heptonolactone	acid, sequestrant; dried soups, instant desserts	
375	nicotinic acid	colour stabiliser and nutrient; bread, flour, breakfast cereals	
380	triammonium citrate	buffer, emulsifying salt; processed cheese	
381	ammonium ferric citrate	dietary iron supplement; bread	
385	calcium disodium ethylenediamine-NNN'N'-tetra-acetate (calcium disodium EDTA)	sequestrant; canned shellfish	
E422	glycerol	humectant, solvent; cake icing, confectionery	148
E450a	disodium dihydrogen diphosphate; trisodium diphosphate; tetrasodium diphosphate; tetra-potassium diphosphate	buffers, sequestrants, emulsifying salts, stabilisers, texturisers, raising agents; used in whipping cream, fish and meat products, bread, processed cheese, cheese spreads, canned vegetables, pork pies, processed chicken and turkey products, beefburgers, sausages, canned ham, cup soups	28, 121–2, 160
E450b	pentasodium triphosphate; pentapotassium tri-phosphate		
E450c	sodium polyphosphates, potassium polyphosphates		
500	sodium carbonate; sodium hydrogen carbonate (bicarbonate of soda); sodium sesquicarbonate	bases, aerating agents, diluents; used in jams, jellies, self-raising flour, wine, cocoa	156
501	potassium carbonate; potassium hydrogen carbonate		

UNDERSTANDING ADDITIVES

Number	Name	Typical food uses	Page
503	ammonium carbonate; ammonium hydrogen carbonate	buffer, aerating agent; cocoa, biscuits	
504	magnesium carbonate	base, anti-caking agent; wafer biscuits, icing sugar	147
507	hydrochloric acid		
508	potassium chloride	gelling agent, salt substitute; table salt replacement	151
509	calcium chloride	firming agent in canned fruit and vegetables	149
510	ammonium chloride	yeast food in bread	156
513	sulphuric acid		
514	sodium sulphate	diluent for colours	156
515	potassium sulphate	salt substitute	
516	calcium sulphate	firming agent and yeast food; bread	
518	magnesium sulphate (Epsom salts)	firming agent	68, 156
524	sodium hydroxide	base; cocoa	147
525	potassium hydroxide	base; sweets	
526	calcium hydroxide	firming agent, neutralising agent; sweets	148
527	ammonium hydroxide	diluent and solvent for food colours, base; cocoa	
528	magnesium hydroxide	base; sweets	
529	calcium oxide	base; sweets	
530	magnesium oxide	anti-caking agent; cocoa products	
535	sodium ferrocyanide	anti-caking agents in salt; crystallisation aids in wine	
536	potassium ferrocyanide		
540	dicalcium diphosphate	buffer, neutralising agent; cheese	
541	sodium aluminium phosphate	acid, raising agent; cake mixes, self-raising flour, biscuits	156
542	edible bone phosphate	anti-caking agent	
544	calcium polyphosphates	emulsifying salt; processed cheese	
545	ammonium polyphosphates	emulsifier, texturiser; frozen chicken	121–2

Number	Name	Typical food uses	Page
636	maltol	flavourings/flavour enhancers used in cakes and biscuits	
637	ethyl maltol		
900	dimethylpolysiloxane	anti-foaming agent	147
901	beeswax	glazing agents used in sugar and chocolate confectionery	
903	carnauba wax		
904	shellac	glazing agent used to wax apples	
905	mineral hydrocarbons	glazing/coating agents used to prevent dried fruit sticking together	148, 150
907	refined microcrystalline wax	release agent; chewing gum	
920	L-cysteine hydrochloride		
924	potassium bromate	flour treatment agents used to improve the texture of bread, cakes and biscuit doughs	147, 157
925	chlorine		
926	chlorine dioxide		
927	azodicarbonamide		
	aluminium potassium sulphate	firming agent; chocolate-coated cherries	150
	2-aminoethanol	base; caustic lye used to peel vegetables	56
	ammonium dihydrogen orthophosphate; diammonium hydrogen orthophosphate	buffer; yeast food	
	ammonium sulphate	yeast food	
	benzoyl peroxide	bleaching agent in flour	147
	butyl stearate	release agent	
	calcium heptonate	firming agent	
	calcium phytate	sequestrant; wine	
	dichlorodifluoromethane	propellant and liquid freezant used to freeze food by immersion	148
	diethyl ether	solvent	
	disodium dihydrogen ethylenediamine-NNN'N'-tetra-acetate (disodium dihydrogen EDTA)	sequestrant; brandy	

Number	Name	Typical food uses	Page
	ethanol (ethyl alcohol)	} solvents used to dilute and carry food colours and flavourings	149, 156
	ethyl acetate		
	glycerol mono-acetate (monoacetin)		
	glycerol di-acetate (diacetin)		
	glycerol tri-acetate (triacetin)		
	glycine	sequestrant, buffer, nutrient	
	hydrogen	} packaging gases	
	nitrogen		
	nitrous oxide	propellant used in aerosol packs of whipped cream	148
	octadecylammonium acetate	anti-caking agent in yeast foods	
	oxygen	packaging gas	
	oxystearin	sequestrant, fat crystallisation inhibitor; salad cream	
	polydextrose	bulking agent, bulk sweetener; reduced and low-calorie foods	20, 56, 147
	propan-1,2-diol (propylene glycol)	} colours and flavourings	
	propan-2-ol (isopropyl alcohol)		
	sodium heptonate	sequestrant; edible oils	
	spermaceti	} release agents	
	sperm oil		
	tannic acid	flavouring, clarifying agent; beer, wine, cider	

Adapted from the leaflet *Food Additives – The Numbers Identified* and reprinted by kind permission of the Ministry of Agriculture, Fisheries and Food.